LAND OF CHOICE

WRITTEN by a Hungarian scholar who himself passed through the vicissitudes of migration and assimilation, this timely study of the movement of Hungarians into Canada has a special value. The author, a graduate of the University of Budapest, taught social history and sociology at the universities of Budapest and Szeged, and had already written considerably on the specific sociological problems he now describes before he entered Canada as an immigrant in 1950.

On Professor Kosa's arrival in North America, his academic interest perforce became practical. Now with a broader insight into the life of the immigrant, he carried out systematic research for the Department of Citizenship and Immigration among his fellow countrymen in Canada. Taking as a sample 112 Hungarian families who had entered the country before 1939, he had a mature immigrant group. Their locale was Toronto and the tobacco district of southwestern Ontario.

This book describes the life and assimilation of these people into a new culture, the problems they faced, and the adjustments made. It will appeal to teachers and students of sociology and anthropology, to the general reader interested in the current Hungarian influx and in the growth of the Canadian community, and to Hungarians who have recently entered Canada. Both timely and scholarly, this is a detailed and careful documentation of what is happening to an important segment of Canadian society.

JOHN KOSA is Assistant Professor of Sociology, Le Moyne College, Syracuse, N.Y.

LAND OF CHOICE

THE HUNGARIANS
IN CANADA

By

John Kosa

UNIVERSITY OF TORONTO PRESS : 1957

IN MEMORIAM

CARISSIMAE

MATRIS ET AVIAE MEAE

Acknowledgments

DURING THE LONG WORK of preparing the present study, I received the selfless assistance of many people. I take this opportunity to express my sincere gratitude to them.

I gratefully acknowledge the grants given for this research by the Canadian Social Science Research Council and the Department of Citizenship and Immigration, Ottawa.

I am greatly indebted to S. D. Clark and Oswald Hall of the University of Toronto, Frank E. Jones of McMaster, Aileen D. Ross of McGill, and Henry Seywerd of the Canadian Citizenship Council, whose encouragement, criticism, and suggestions were of constant assistance during my work. Frank M. Vicroy of the University of Louisville gave all the necessary help in the statistical part of the study.

For many details of the Hungarian background I am indebted to Imre Bernolak of the Department of Labour, Ottawa, Stephen Borsody of Chatham College, Robert Major of New York City, Julius Rezler of Loyola University, and Stephen Ullmann of the University of Leeds, England. For critical reading of some of the chapters I am obliged to Claude W. Thompson and Harold H. Potter of Sir George Williams College as well as to Hugh H. Davis and Raymond A. Wiley of Le Moyne College.

My former student, Kurt Jonassohn, helped greatly in the preparation of the manuscript, charts, and statistical material. I owe particular gratitude to Arthur Candib of Sir George Williams College. With his knowledge of the problems of immigration and with the care he gave to the present study he could have written another, and perhaps better, book.

Finally, I wish to express my thanks to those Canadian Hungarians, over 200 in number, who during the long interviews patiently answered my questions. Their friendly co-operation and hospitality gave me sympathetic encouragement and made my research work a pleasant undertaking.

J. K.

Contents

Tables and Charts

LAND OF CHOICE

CHAPTER I

INTRODUCTION

ONE OUT OF EVERY SEVEN PERSONS in Canada is an immigrant, and the difference between foreign-born and native-born is more than a matter of words. Native-born people inherited their country and own it by a right of birth. They were reared in that country and adopted its way of life through a natural course. They move in its milieu with the ease of being at home and have no special problems of how to be a Canadian. For the immigrant, however, Canada is a land of choice. He selected it because life in the old country was poor, and sometimes intolerable, while Canada offered better opportunities, greater freedom or a more promising future. He selected Canada out of free will; yet it was difficult to renounce his old country.

The immigrant, walking ashore at Halifax or Montreal, brought with him not only the bundles of his material possessions, but also the culture of his native country—its language, its customs of family life, clothing, housing, cooking, and working. When disembarking, he found a strange, sometimes even frightening land where the culture of the old country could not be used. The land of choice offered bright chances, but posed high requirements. The immigrant had to establish a new existence, find a gratifying job, build up a home, found a family. Furthermore, he had to adopt the culture of the new country, its language, customs, way of life. He faced a difficult personal problem. He had to work and to adjust himself since only adjustment opened up the new country.

The land of choice presented a bold challenge, and the usual responses the immigrants gave to this challenge were adjustment and assimilation. Nevertheless, people responded in their own ways. Some immigrants overcame the personal difficulties with a rare talent, and earned public praise for their extraordinary success. Others succumbed to the difficulties, failed to adjust, and left the country in disappointment. The majority, however, fell somewhere between the two extremes. The average immigrant established himself, became Canadianized, and his personal fate melted into that of the average Canadians. This was a slow process of subtle changes, a matter of many years, or a man's life. It manifested itself in the small details of daily life so gradually that not even the immigrant, immersed as he was in his regular routine, noticed it. However, if a cross-section of the immigrants is taken, and their fortunes are examined over a long period, the changes stand out conspicuously. The present study aims to trace the changes of adjustment within a group of Hungarian immigrants in Canada.

Hungarians are one of the "small peoples" of central Europe, numbering between ten and twelve millions. Among the ethnic groups of America, too, they form but a small group. In the United States in 1950 the "Hungarian stock" (comprising the foreign-born and the native-born of foreign or mixed parentage) counted 705,102, less than one-half of one per cent of the population. Such a figure, however, includes a certain number of people whose ties with anything Hungarian are either weak or no longer existent. In Canada, the census of 1951 found 60,460 residents of Hungarian origin. The figure, which includes Canadian-born descendants of Hungarian immigrants, represented less than one-half of one per cent of the Canadian population.

Hungarian immigrants began to arrive in Canada in the 1880's when the Prairies were opened up and the Dominion initiated a new, vigorous immigration policy. They settled mainly on the homesteads of the Prairies, particularly in the present Province of Saskatchewan, but they were few in number as long as the door to the United States stood open. In 1911 there were fewer than 10,000 in Canada.[1] World War I interrupted European immigration, and when it was resumed after the war it showed many new patterns. The United States restricted immigration, and the small quota allotted to the Hungarians practically barred them. Now Canada became the most important destination of Hungarian migrants, with Latin America and France following her in importance. In the decade 1921–30, 28,000 Hungarians came to Canada, and their number would have been greater had the Hungarian government not imposed severe restrictions upon emigration. Immigrants of this second wave, instead of going west, settled in the industrial areas of eastern Canada, particularly in Ontario, which now became the centre of Canadian Hungarians. There, as Table I shows, their number grew steadily, although the depression slowed down the influx of newcomers. World War II brought it to a standstill, and when peace was restored, a new wandering of peoples began.

[1]The Canadian census of 1901 and 1911 enumerated the Hungarians together with Lithuanians and Moravians, and the two latter groups cannot be subtracted now. Accurate data on the number of Hungarians are available only from 1921 on.

TABLE I

POPULATION OF HUNGARIAN ORIGIN, CANADA AND PROVINCES
1921–1951

	1921	1931	1941	1951
Total—Canada	13,181	40,582	54,598	60,460
Quebec	89	4,018	4,134	4,127
Ontario	1,737	13,786	22,039	28,182
Manitoba	828	1,955	2,418	2,326
Saskatchewan	8,946	13,363	14,576	12,470
Alberta	1,045	5,502	7,892	7,794
British Columbia	343	1,313	2,893	4,948

European refugees asked for admission to the American countries, and from the beginning of 1946 to the end of 1953 Canada admitted almost 12,000 immigrants of Hungarian origin, most of them refugees.

Political changes in the homeland affected not only the flow, but also the social composition of immigration. Up to the 1930's an estimated 90 per cent of the immigrants hailed from the poor classes of Hungary, especially from the agrarian proletariat. They were the children of the landless peasantry or of the "dwarf holders" whose property was too small to provide a livelihood for their families. They were compelled by the critical social problems of the country, by poverty, the system of great landed estates, and the social and political inequality of the classes, to seek new homes on the other side of the Atlantic. After 1945, however, those who came to America had been uprooted by the political disasters that befell Hungary during and after the war. Whether those people were Jews persecuted by the government, members of the ruling class, men in the learned professions or businessmen standing aloof from politics, they represented the upper classes of the country. It is estimated that the majority of the refugees were recruited from the middle class, a term which, as used in Hungary, describes a social group rather similar to the upper-middle or upper class in America.

In those European countries such as Hungary where the remnants of feudalism survived up to the end of World War II the differences between the social classes were great indeed. The classes were separated by formal, conspicuous barriers, and the entire behaviour and appearance of a middle-class person were visibly different from those of a peasant. Such a difference survived immigration. The fortunes and behaviour of the Hungarian immigrant in America can be understood only in the light of his social origin as expressed in terms of classes. The present study investigates the life of the old, poor-class immigrants.[2]

The methods used in our research were established during a preliminary study of the knowledge of English among immigrants.[3] On the basis of the experience gained then it was decided to study a sample group selected as follows:

1. The sample consisted of immigrants who came as adults (16 years of age and over) from the poor classes of Hungary. In Hungarian society class origin determined education. Our sample had what was the typical schooling of the poor class—four to eight years in the grammar school of the old country, but no formal education in Canada.

2. All immigrants selected had come to Canada prior to 1939 and had reached a certain degree of adjustment and assimilation. The sample constituted a "mature" immigrant group with twenty-four years as its median length of Canadian residence in 1951, and in fact showed a close approach to the respective distribution of the Hungarian immigrant population of Canada according to period of immigration, as presented by the census of 1951.

3. The sample was restricted to residents of the Province of Ontario. In 1951, 54 per cent of the Hungarian-born population of Canada lived in Ontario, the rest being scattered in all but the Maritime Provinces. The Hungarians in Ontario undoubtedly differ in many respects from their compatriots in the other provinces. However, practical considerations involved in the research project made such a restriction imperative.

4. Care was taken that the rural-urban distribution of the sample should accord with that of the Hungarian immigrant population. In one respect, however, the exactness of the sampling can be questioned. For practical reasons, the urban population of the sample was selected from the metropolitan area of Toronto, and the farming population from the tobacco belt of Ontario. Since it is generally considered that the immigrants in Ontario are financially better off than those of some

[2]Cf. C. A. Macartney, *Hungary* (London, 1934), and *Hungary and Her Successors* (Oxford, 1937); John Eppstein, ed., *Hungary* (Cambridge, 1945); Hugh Seton Watson, *Eastern Europe between the Wars* (Cambridge, 1945); *Handbooks: Hungary* (United Kingdom Foreign Office, London, 1945). Concerning the social stratification in Hungary see Gyula Szekfü, *Három nemzedék és ami utána következik* (Budapest, 1935); John Kosa, *Magyar rendiség és osztálytársadalom* (Budapest, 1942), and "Hungarian Society in the Time of the Regency," *Journal of Central European Affairs*, XVI (October 1956).

[3]John Kosa, "The Knowledge of English among Hungarian Immigrants in Canada," in I. Bernolak, A. R. Boyd, *et al.*, *Immigrants in Canada* (Montreal, 1955).

other provinces, the financial status of the whole Hungarian stock is very likely somewhat less favourable than that of the sample as detailed in chapter III.

5. Care was taken that the religious affiliations, with respect to Catholics and Protestants, should be representative.

6. The data of the census, as will be explained in chapter IV, could not be accepted as a safe guide concerning the marital status of Hungarian immigrants. However, from consultation with several Hungarian priests and ministers we believe that the rate of married and single persons in the sample is not misleading concerning the entire old immigrant stock.

The field work was begun in 1950 and finished in August 1953, and thus started before the 1951 census was taken. Sampling began with the aid of conjectures based on the 1941 census and other data at our disposal. As the figures of the 1951 census became available, the necessary corrections in the objectives of the sampling were made, and finally 112 men, or rather family units, were selected to make up the final sample. The sample thus established is believed to be representative, with certain qualifications, of the old Hungarian stock.

We contacted the 112 respondents not as strangers, but as friends. We were either introduced to them by a friend or relative of theirs, or we met them before the first interview at a Hungarian home or club. Such an approach assured the sincere co-operation of the respondents in many delicate matters.

Each respondent was asked to relate his life history, notably the circumstances of his emigration and his experience in Canada. Such broad questioning gave him liberty to tell his story rather lengthily and not only to relate the facts, but also to give his opinions and comments, the latter furnishing an important part of the present study. The informality of the interviews permitted us to ask all those questions that seemed to be necessary—for example, to clarify vague statements.

The original plan called for interviews with men only, since in the Hungarian peasantry the man is the head of the family and makes the important decisions, such as that concerning emigration. The men formed the basis of the sample group, and the statistical data of the study, unless otherwise specified, refer to the 112 men. Very soon, however, it was found that the wives took a great interest in the research and volunteered the family histories on their side. Frequently, the length of their stories greatly exceeded those of their husbands. In this way valuable material amply used in the informative part of this study was obtained. The children of the immigrants, the second-generation people, were not interviewed. However, some voluntary information furnished by them was used to sketch their role and position in the immigrant family.

This procedure usually required two to three sittings for the relating of a family history, after which certain additional personal data had to be collected. Thus, the families were visited at least three times, and some of them, because of our friendly relations, more often. Moreover, the respondents had friends and relatives in the sample or among our acquaintances not included in the sample. Accordingly, it was possible to check the data the respondents gave or to obtain further information. In a closed community (such as an ethnic group which a person from the out-group cannot enter without serious difficulties) gossip and rumour must circulate. We heard much of this, and when interpreted with necessary caution, it gave us additional valuable material.

Beside the interviews, participation in the life of the Hungarian group yielded further field material. The author, being a "greenie" (recent immigrant) from Hungary, was accepted and helped in his research just as any newcomer would be. On the other hand, he was often consulted on such problems as translating, tax returns, or even business deals. The gay social life of the Hungarians, their visiting habits and fondness of parties, furnished excellent occasions to observe their life. The interviews were mostly carried out in the evening or during week-ends and holidays. Since this is the usual time for friendly visits, the interviews were often followed, or interrupted, by guests dropping in. The long talks and lively debates, the formal and informal parties, revealed essential traits of the group life and provided a supplement to the interviews.

Hungarians other than those included in the sample were interviewed on one point or another. Priests, ministers, some ethnic leaders and educated persons, both immigrants and Canadian-born, added many helpful data.

In addition to this field work the Hungarian press of both Canada and the United States proved to be another fruitful source of information. We were able to use a rich but incomplete private collection of Hungarian newspapers published during the depression. In the years from 1950 to 1954 we regularly followed the Hungarian papers. Although the study draws extensively upon this material, none of the papers is cited in the footnotes, in order to preserve the anonymity of persons dealt with in this study. For the same reason, all names, initials, titles, ranks and similar data which would reveal identity are kept fictitious.

The field study turned out to be something like a discovery—discovery of a small world in itself, the Hungarian-Canadian group, which has its own characteristics, differing from both the majority population of Canada and the society of Hungary. This particular world is rapidly changing, dying out in the natural cycle of human life, becoming adjusted and assimilated to the Canadian environment. Within a short time its picture will be quite different from that drawn in the following pages. Its present state, however, mirrors the average immigrant's response to the challenges of the land of choice.

CHAPTER II

MIGRATION AND THE SIB SYSTEM

THOSE YOUNG PEASANTS IN HUNGARY who took it upon themselves to emigrate hardly knew the world outside their native country. The majority of them had never lived or worked in a large city, and few of them had ever visited another country. For such people it was a bold undertaking, a jump into the darkness, to leave behind their well-known birthplace and seek a new life in another hemisphere. Having made the decision to emigrate, they had to face many obstacles. Hungarian authorities were reluctant to issue passports; other embarrassments were caused by the emigrants' ignorance and poverty, and the uncertainty of their future; some personal tragedies emerged such as the reluctance of wife or bride to emigrate. Under such circumstances some people changed their minds and abandoned the plan. Those who did emigrate had to be moved by motives strong enough to counterbalance the hardships of the undertaking and the timidity of unsophisticated people.

The great European emigration is explained by several factors among which the general increase of population is an important one.[1] The overpopulated areas of Europe sent out their surplus into other, underpopulated continents. However, overpopulation is a relative factor, relative to the social, economic and other conditions of a given society at a given time, and does not account for the whole extent of migratory movements. Before 1914 Hungary was less densely populated, but sent forth more emigrants, than after 1920. Some countries (Poland, Lithuania, Russia) were less densely populated than Hungary, but their contribution to American immigration was heavier.[2]

The system of large estates was another decisive factor in Hungarian as well as in Polish and Irish emigration. In Hungary, the rural proletariat had practically no chance of advancement or of acquiring sufficient land, and young people had to leave their native villages

[1]Donald R. Taft, *Human Migration* (New York, 1936), chap. v; Julius Isaac, *Economics of Migration* (London, 1947); Eugene M. Kulischer, *Europe on the Move* (New York, 1948).
[2]Aloys Kovács, *The Development of the Population of Hungary* (Budapest, 1920).

and look for a livelihood elsewhere. However, some counties where the rule of large estates was less oppressive (Nyir, Csanád, Pest) had a greater share in emigration than some where the hold of large estate owners was firmer (Transdanubia).

The rapid progress of transportation techniques stimulated the migration of masses. Railways and steamships rendered travel faster, safer and cheaper than ever before. The propaganda of American steamship and railway companies reached the remotest villages in Hungary, and in the decades of mass emigration the agents of transportation companies even approached the peasants in their homes. However, a bill passed in the Hungarian parliament in 1903 made "inducement to emigration" a criminal offence, and the role of emigration agents gradually declined.[3]

Beside these general factors, common in many European countries, specific conditions in Hungary were also an incentive. Emigration from Hungary began right after the abolition of serfdom (1848) and was tied up with a slow transformation of society. The old feudal system before 1848 bound the peasant to the glebe. It was an unjust order, but it imposed a great stability upon society. Large masses of the peasantry could not move freely, but they enjoyed a certain primitive security within this system. They were sure of subsistence and could expect support from the landlord and village community in time of need. It was rightly said at that time that "nobody can starve in his home village." With the abolition of serfdom and the removal of legal bondage, the former serfs were free to move. At the same time the obligations of the landlords were renounced, and those of the village community weakened, depriving the freed serf of a great part of his previous security. Hence, this great social change opened up a new, migratory mobility.

Class society gave way to faster upward social mobility. At the same time it promoted a new attitude toward social ascent. Now, everybody

[3]Concerning Hungarian emigration see Lóránt Hegedüs, *A magyarok kivándorlása Amerikába* (Budapest, 1899); Gusztáv Thirring, *A magyaroszági kivándorlás* (Budapest, 1904); *A kivándorlás. A Magyar Gyáriparosok Országos Szövetsége által tartott országos ankét tárgyalásai* (Budapest, 1907); Pál Farkas, *Az amerikai kivándorlás* (Budapest, 1907); Bertalan Neményi, *A magyar nép állapota és az amerikai kivándorlás* (Budapest, 1911); Imre Kovács, *Kivándorlás* (Budapest, 1937); John Kosa, *Die ungarische Kolonisationsfrage* (Budapest, 1939). Concerning Hungarian immigration cf. Joseph Remenyi, "The Hungarians," in H. P. Fairchild, ed., *Immigrant Backgrounds* (New York, 1927); Andrew A. Marchbin, "Early Emigration from Hungary to Canada," *Slavonic and East European Review*, XIII (July 1934); Francis R. Brown and Joseph S. Roucek, *One America* (New York, 1948); R. A. Schermerhorn, *These Our People* (Boston, 1949).

who made money could proceed into a higher social stratum, sometimes even into the highest ones. The new mentality approved almost every method of making money, and the ways that led to wealth were eagerly sought. They could not be found in the village community with its large estate and poorly paid charwork, and the cities could absorb only a small part of the rural population. Under such circumstances America, with its high wages and good opportunities, became indeed "the land of promise." As knowledge about America spread in the Hungarian villages, more and more people betook themselves to the adventure of trying their luck in the New World. However, emigration still remained a bold undertaking, and only the poor, who had nothing to lose, launched into it.

Thus the transition from a feudal into a class society furnished the framework for mass emigration. But the details of the process were determined by a basic institution of Hungarian society—the familial ties of the sib system. Table II shows the important role "relatives"

TABLE II

ASSISTANCE IN IMMIGRATION RECEIVED OR GIVEN BY A
GROUP OF 112 HUNGARIAN IMMIGRANTS IN CANADA

	Number	Percentage
Received financial help in immigration from relatives	62	55.4
Received help of other kind in immigration from relatives	25	22.3
Received no help	25	22.3
Gave financial help in immigration to relatives	39	34.8
Gave help of other kind in immigration to relatives	16	14.3
Tried to give help in immigration to relatives	51	45.5
Gave no help	6	5.4
Total	112	100.0

played in immigration. Three out of every four immigrants in the sample came to Canada with aid received from "relatives." Almost every Hungarian in Canada gave help or tried to help relatives in their immigration. In many cases their efforts could not achieve the desired result because the political system of Regency which ruled the country from 1920 to 1944 clamped down on emigration; then the war, and later the Communist system, practically stopped emigration from Hungary. But in the whole group of 112, only 2 men neither received help nor tried to help their relatives in immigration. Both can be regarded as extreme types of the maladjusted immigrant whose failures in other fields of life will be analysed later.

To understand the importance of familial ties, it must be pointed out that the word "family" has two meanings in Hungarian. It connotes, first, the unity of parents and children, and the following pages will use it consistently in this sense. In a second meaning it describes the sib, that is, a wide circle of relatives which includes aunts, uncles, cousins, sometimes of a very remote degree, in-laws with their families, and, as an essential part, godparents with their families.[4] All members of the sib are called "relatives," although many of them are not related by blood.

The Hungarian sib system has a long history. From the early Middle Ages, a patrilinear clanship system existed in the Hungarian nobility. Clans had a conspicuous role in national policy, and alliances of powerful clans made up those political factions which ruled over the country. Alliances between the clans were sealed with marriage, and the in-laws, later even the godparents, became regarded as relatives. The old clans disappeared in the fourteenth century, but a new nobility emerged which still endeavoured to establish advantageous marriage relations with other families. In such a way alliances of more or less related families were built up, sibs which inherited the political importance of the clans. Later on, perhaps in the sixteenth and seventeenth centuries, the sib system was taken over by the burgher and peasant classes, and it has been an important characteristic of Hungarian society up to our time.[5]

In the sib system, as it existed in recent centuries, the families of the sib did not live together (as the case was in the "enlarged family" of the Slavic peasant societies), but instead maintained their independence and separate homes, and were often scattered over neighbouring villages—some middle-class sibs, over the whole country. Moreover, the sib was never articulated according to blood relationship. Some distant relatives were strongly attached, some near ones left out. Endogamy in the sib was not only possible, but even encouraged in order to keep the fortune "among relatives." Consequently,

[4]The Hungarian language has different names to denote "sib" (család, atyafiság, nemzetség, rokonság, had, sógorság, komaság), but "family" is the word used most generally.

[5]János Karácsonyi, *A magyar nemzetségek a XIV. sz. közepéig* (3 vols., Budapest, 1900–3); Péter Ágoston, *A magyar világi nagybirtok története* (Budapest, 1913). The historical role played by the sib is well analysed by Gyula Szekfü, in his *Magyar történet* (3rd ed., Budapest, 1935), vols. III–V.

members of the sib were often bound together by two- or three-fold ties.

In spite of loose blood relationship, the sib was strongly linked by unwritten customs and mutual obligations which regulated the whole range of life. Among customs, the rituals of marriage and burial and the birthday and nameday celebrations[6] were most conspicuous. The essential tie, however, was a moral obligation to help one another in every way. The members of the sib were supposed in every need to give and receive help—labour, money or moral support. Novelist Kálmán Mikszáth described a case where more than twenty families contributed for long years to send a talented son of the sib into higher schools. Burdens fell more heavily upon the richer or more successful members. If someone achieved high position in politics or the civil service, it was his duty to "take care" of his sib through patronage. Positions in local or national politics, in the civil service, and even in some sectors of business life were often allotted to sib members and were controlled by alliances of friendly sibs. Hence, individual success was extremely difficult; it was rather the whole sib as a unit that ascended the social ladder. The sib determined the individual's social status, and a "good sib" gave higher prestige than money.

Although the sib played a conspicuous part in public life, it was an informal organization without any definite leadership; its life was directed by customary co-operation. Sometimes the opinion of a successful, wise or old member carried special weight and influenced other members, but he could not give commands and could not direct families other than his own. Because of the informality, the sib had no special name. It was referred to as "our family" by the members, or "their relatives" by non-members. The sib ensured co-operation and regulated the private life of members through old established customs.[7] According to custom "it was a shame" if a member of the sib forgot his obligations. There were many "ought to's" and "must not's" in family life. The lore of the sib system, its etiquette, customs and genealogy made up a conspicuous part of the education every child received from his family. Such an education, together with certain

⁶Nameday is the day when the person's first name is "in the calendar," that is, when the Catholic church commemorates his patron saint. In Hungary it was celebrated by Catholics and Protestants as well.

⁷The most important collections of the Hungarian customs are Péter Apor, *Metamorphosis Transylvaniae* (Budapest, 1863); Matthias Bél, *Notitia Hungariae* (4 vols., 1735–42); Béla Radvánszky, *Magyar családélet és háztartás a XVI. és XVII. században* (3 vols., Budapest, 1879–86); Károly Tagányi, *Lebende Rechtsgewohnheiten and ihre Sammlung in Ungarn* (Berlin, 1922); Károly Viski, *Hungarian Peasant Customs* (Budapest, 1932).

familistic sanctions, were effective enough to keep up the system for many centuries.

If an individual launched an undertaking, he could always count on the help of his sib. This help was particularly important in the case of emigration, for people from the poor classes could never have financed the cost of emigration by themselves. Sometimes five to ten families contributed to "send out" one person to America. One informant who came to Canada about 1910 told the following story: "At that time, emigration cost 250 Crowns. I saved for a long time, but could not manage more than 120 Crowns. Then Uncle B. gave 40 Crowns, and Uncle C. 25, and some other relatives helped it up to 200 Crowns. But I was still short, and I thought I must wait another year. Then Cousin D. arrived for a visit and put down the money I needed."

Another informant tried for a long time to figure out a way to get the necessary money. Although he had a rich uncle, the uncle was "wicked," and would not help his relatives. Finding no other way out, the young man visited his uncle one night to ask for help. He described Canada as a country "where you can find gold at one inch from the top of the soil; where you can make a dollar an hour; where farmers live in better homes than counts in Hungary." This plea moved the uncle's heart, and he offered to lend the necessary amount. In many other cases sib members residing in America advanced or paid the costs of emigration.[8]

The immigrant arrived in Canada with obligations towards his sib in the old country. He considered it his duty to return the aid received. As soon as he found a steady job, he started to send "home" his savings; as soon as he became settled, he tried to "bring out" his relatives.[9] It was generally held that "it is enough if one son goes overseas"; in other words, custom ruled that the immigrant should not be joined by his brother but rather by a son of another sib family. After a time in Canada, therefore, the immigrant encouraged and assisted in the immigration, not of his brother, but of a sib member such as a cousin, a brother-in-law, or the son of his godparents. Now the sib had two members in Canada, and with common effort they "helped over" a third or even fourth relative. As a result, a special

[8]Irish immigrants often had their passage fare paid by friends in America. Cf. Stanley C. Johnson, *A History of Emigration from the United Kingdom to North America* (London, 1913), p. 70.

[9]A similar attitude was observed among Polish immigrants by W. I. Thomas and Florian Znaniecki, *The Polish Peasant in Europe and America* (2nd ed., New York, 1927), p. 1493.

familistic articulation came to exist in the Hungarian ethnic group; almost every Hungarian has relatives in Canada, but few of them have brothers here. The agrarian proletariat, with its strong sib system, contributed heavily to immigration, but the urban proletariat, where the sib system had broken down, fell proportionally behind.

The history of the sib Nagy, shown in Chart 1, illustrates how immigration followed the sib line. During a period of fifty-odd years the sib managed to promote the immigration of seventeen members. Its first members pioneered in the Prairie Provinces, the two lastcomers were post-war D.P.'s. In the history of the whole sib there has been one case only where an immigrant was followed by his brother. On the other hand, immigration was promoted in several instances by other than the nearest relative. Ties of intermarriage, godparentship, or personal affections often took precedence over blood ties. It should be noted that the Nagy sib with its seventeen member families in Canada is exceptionally large, the largest one we have met. The average Hungarian sib in Canada consists of three to five families.

If at the time of his arrival the immigrant had relatives in Canada, his burden was lightened through their aid. He received his passage and his immigration permit from them. At the moment of his arrival he could expect even more help. It was a strict obligation upon sib members to guard the newcomer, to teach him Canadian ways and to provide him with quarters and a job. If the newcomer was single, he took up residence with a sib family, and even in the case of families the sharing of residence was widely practised.

In every case, the families of a sib preferred to live near one another. Such a tendency seemed to be an important factor in the interprovincial migration of Hungarians. When one family moved from the Prairies to Ontario and found the situation favourable, it was soon followed by another family of the sib. When the first Hungarian farmers appeared in the tobacco county of Western Ontario in the 1930's, they were soon joined by relatives. If the members of the sib were separated, as in the case of the Nagys, they did their best to keep the sib together through correspondence and visiting.

The same clannishness could be observed in the field of labour. The older immigrant helped the newcomer into a job similar to his own, and sib people liked to work together. Factory workers in Toronto usually endeavoured to bring their relatives into the shop where they were working. The sib stuck together even in certain fields of independent business. When one immigrant became successful in landscape gardening, he was soon followed by two members of his sib. The first

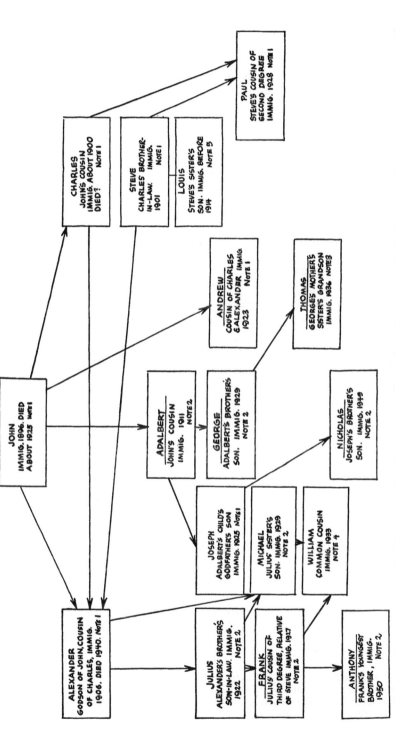

CHART 1. Immigration of the Nagy sib to Canada. Arrows indicate the help given; underlined names indicate those persons who still maintain the sib system.

NOTES: 1. Lived or is living in Prairie Provinces. 2. Living in Ontario. 3. Living in U.S.A. 4. Recent fate unknown. 5. Died soon after in accident.

one, not afraid of competition, gave every help to these relatives in establishing themselves. He instructed them, lent tools or truck, and proudly boasted that in a short time "the family will have in their hands" the gardening of a certain suburb of Toronto.

Sib means mutual aid, and it was every immigrant's best interest to build up a large and powerful sib. Success in Canada was easy for those who had a "good sib," but hard for those who were "alone." The well-to-do families in our sample usually had a good sized sib comprising other well-to-do families. On the other hand, the majority of poor Hungarians were either single or had renounced their sib ties. The immigrants themselves are well aware of these facts. When speaking of the financial success of a certain Hungarian, one informant remarked: "He would never have reached that without his brother-in-law." When a rather unpopular person was elected president of a club, somebody commented: "It was not for him, but for his sib."

The new sibs that came to exist in Canada were extended branches of old ones living in Hungary, and the relations of the two lines were regulated by customary obligations. They were frequently exchanging letters and sending birthday, nameday or Christmas greetings. In addition to letters, money and gifts were sent back. All immigrant groups did the same, and the money received from America was an important item of national income in the countries of emigration.[10] In Hungary it was a prominent factor in the social ascent of whole sibs. In certain counties, for example in Nyir, the wealth of entire villages was attributed to relatives in America, and in the poverty-ridden years following the two world wars, "American uncles" saved many families from becoming utterly destitute.

The Hungarians in Canada conscientiously discharged their duties in this respect. One woman said: "We could have bought another rooming house on the money we sent home." Another one stated that such expenditures "ran into thousands and thousands." At the time of our research, the most important business centring around the Hungarian group was that of "travel agencies" which handled the money orders and gift parcels sent to Hungary. One of these agents estimated that "at the boom of the business," early in 1952, every month 40,000 parcels were sent from Canada to Hungary or to Hungarian refugees living in Europe.

[10]The earnings of the Rumanian immigrants in America were sent back and helped poor Rumanians in Transylvania to buy land. Max Handman, "Conflict and Equilibrium in a Border Area," in E. B. Reuter, ed., Race and Culture Contacts (New York, 1934), p. 97.

These estimates seem exaggerated, for the years spent in Canada inevitably loosened the ties with the sib in Hungary. The last war and the Communist régime that followed suspended or halted correspondence. The Hungarian branch of the sib has been for many years unable to discharge its great duty, that is, to send out new immigrants. As a result, the immigrant became more independent of his old-country sib; the feeling of his obligations weakened, the material help given lessened. Many respondents stated: "In old times we used to send home everything. Lately we do it rarely." One woman explained the same idea with more details: "After such a long time, you don't feel the same way towards those people. You haven't seen them for more than twenty years. Many of them have died, and there are many children whom I have never seen and never shall see."

When the immigrant arrived in Canada, he had a life plan conceived by the sib—to save money in America, buy land in the old country, return and enjoy life there. He had no intention of settling down in Canada permanently. He sent his savings back to Hungary where his father or brother, acting as trustees, saved or invested these sums. As time passed and the years spent in Canada grew into decades, the attitude of the immigrant changed. He became independent from his relatives in the old country and he changed over to an individual life plan. He wanted to possess property in Canada and went into farming or the rooming-house business in order to make money faster. Gradually he postponed, or abandoned, the return to the old country. His life plan was no longer shaped by the customs of the sib, but by Canadian patterns. As he gave up the ties to the old sib, he began to regard Canada as his final home. Decades were necessary to bring forth such a transformation, but the final change in the life plan signified the adjustment of the immigrant to his new country.

But though the ties with Hungary loosened, the sib in Canada stuck together. The hardships of the new country hammered it into a forceful unit, into the main protective system of the immigrants which, giving aid, stood by all the time. There were occasional quarrels and resentments among sib members, but quarrels do take place in every family. A few persons "pulled off" from the sib, but such "ungratefulness" might happen in Hungary also. As a general rule, however, the immigrant generation rigorously maintained the sib organization.

A sib that can count many members or that has a strong leader is apt to survive for a long time; one of them had a firm hold even over the fifth-generation people. Its head, a Canadian-born son of one of the first Hungarian settlers, was brought up in the pioneer time of the Prairies and cherished the old, Hungarian patterns of life. Having made some fortune and possessing great common sense, he led his sib with a certain patriarchal authority. On Sundays the sib gathered in his home, and the old man never forgot to stress before them the importance of Hungarian customs.

As a rule, however, the sib system is doomed to die out with the first generation. Members of the second generation acquire, through their Canadian education, the value system and patterns of life which are general in Canada, and the essence of the sib system is strange and incomprehensible to them.[11] They accept the family in its American form, as a small unit of parents and children. They do not understand how distant relatives can interfere with somebody's life. They accept the American concept of success in which the family is not necessarily a factor in social ascent. They want to make their own success, alone and for themselves. They do not count on the help of relatives and reject the heavy burden of aiding the same relatives. For them the idea of mutual aid, an essential element in the sib organization, is completely lost.

The parents wish to maintain the sib and employ some coercion. In one case a 16-year-old second-generation boy left his home when the sib was gathering and behaved himself "unbecomingly" towards his relatives. When he returned home late that night, he was upbraided by his parents, and instead of the dishes of fête he was given only sandwiches for supper. As his mother explained to him: "If your family is not good for you, the family dishes should not be good either." Parental coercion and persuasion, however, are unable to cope with the impact of the Canadian environment, and as the second-generation people grow up, they stay away from the sib. A teen-aged boy summed up his problem in an unusually sharp tone: "Daddy keeps on talking about Aunt So-and-So and Uncle This-and-That, and there are always aunts and uncles, and I have so many of them that I cannot keep their names in mind. But why should I have more relatives than anybody else? Who would do anything for an aunt in this country? Daddy thinks too much of his relatives."

Moreover, the second generation has not learned properly, and does not appreciate, those elaborate customs which regulate the life of the

[11]As a similar phenomenon, an old Chinese complained that his son "not understand our family [i.e. clan] in China." N. S. Hayner and C. N. Reynolds, "Chinese Family Life in America," *American Sociological Review*, II (Oct. 1937), pp. 630–7.

sib. Since they do not use "Hungarian calendars," they forget the namedays, those festive rituals when everyone must greet the person celebrating his nameday. The second generation, finally, does not know personally the sib in the old country and has no special feeling for far-away relatives. Their attitude towards Canadian sib members, although friendly, differs essentially from the Hungarian pattern. Social life was organized there on the basis of sib, and, often, a youth's best friend was one of his uncles, a person twenty years his senior. American society, particularly the youth, is organized more sharply into age groups, and the cohesion of age groups, such as gangs, is often stronger than that of families.[12] Consequently, those of the second generation stick to their age group and select their friends among Canadians instead of sib members. As they become independent in life, they lose their interest in the "relatives," and after the death of their parents they tend to withdraw from the remaining sib, a decisive step in their assimilation. When saying farewell to the sib, they say farewell to the Hungarian ethnic group as well. From this time on they can be regarded as Canadians only.[13]

[12]As it was observed among second-generation Italian immigrants in Boston by William F. Whyte, *Street Corner Society* (Chicago, 1943), pp. 255–9.

[13]Familistic organizations similar to the Hungarian sib can be found in many European societies. The kinship patterns in Germany, Poland, and Italy bear a particular resemblance to those in Hungary.

CHAPTER III

FINANCIAL SUCCESS AND STRATIFICATION

IN THE LIFE of the poor Hungarian peasant, money played a rather inconspicuous role. Labourers on the large estate were paid in crops rather than in money; poor farmers clung to their inherited "dwarf farms" even when cultivation became uneconomic; and the individual's status was based not so much on his wealth as on such unmarketable factors as his sib's reputation, his form of life, or his title and rank. The immigrant left the old country to escape from the poverty of a feudalistic bondage.[1] He desired access to the money easily available in America, and he endeavoured to compete for financial advancement under the favourable circumstances offered by America. His life in the New World came to be measured in terms of his financial success.

The data obtained from the sample group permitted an estimate of the success of the immigrants in their competition for money. Income, however, could not be used as a measure of financial success since farmers' or small businessmen's income often cannot be determined accurately. Moreover, income alone does not indicate whether the immigrant achieved his goal—the accumulation of savings. Therefore, we tried to determine the wealth owned by the group, particularly that part of the wealth which was vested in real estate or business undertakings. The Hungarian "peasant etiquette" deems it unbecoming that a person should disclose his income or debts; but, fortunately enough, the etiquette is less strict concerning real estate ownership. In the closed community of the ethnic group the members seemed to be well informed of one another's properties. They gave information about their own holdings, and the statements could be checked by their friends and relatives.

By this means we established the properties (farm, house, cottage, lot, business site) owned by members of the group as well as their

[1]Concerning the financial circumstances of the Hungarian agricultural population see József Nádujfalvy, *A gazdasági munkabérek* (Budapest, 1942); János Szeberthy-Szeiberth, *Munkanélküliség és napszámbér a mezögazdaságban* (Budapest, 1939); András Heller, *Föld és munkabér* (Budapest, 1939).

purchase price. Such raw figures, however, had to be corrected because real estate values in Ontario had been showing an uninterrupted increase during the previous fifteen years.[2] For all properties acquired in or after 1949 the purchase price was accepted as basis of valuation which then was corrected with the value of improvements and the usual allowance for depreciation. For properties acquired prior to 1949, two to four persons who were intimate with the land values were asked to give a fair valuation. In the case of discrepancies the conservative estimate was taken. Since such estimates included both improvements and depreciation, no special correction was made.

Because of etiquette, mortgages and other liabilities, as well as bank deposits and other assets, could not be ascertained and were omitted. Assets worth less than $5,000 such as cars, trucks, home furniture and other personal belongings were not taken into account. In certain business undertakings (gardening, plumbing, rooming-house business) the total value of business assets fell under the limit of $5,000 and was left out. Similar business assets over the limit of $5,000 were, however, included. Since the estimates were given in round thousand dollars, the computed figures were rounded up or down to the nearest $1,000 value.

The final figures show that, at about the end of 1952, the aggregate wealth of the 112 family units could be estimated at $3,526,000, or an average $31,000 for each family unit. To picture the real distribution of wealth within the immigrant group, the 112 families were arranged in three classes. Those with properties less than $15,000 were called "poor"; those with properties over $15,000 and under $35,000, "medium"; and those with properties over $35,000, "well-to-do." As Table III shows, one-third of the group qualified for the well-to-do class, almost one-half of it reached the level of the medium class, and less than one-fifth of the group had less than $15,000.

It has already been pointed out, however, that the sample group should not be regarded as representative of the financial status of Hungarian immigrants in Canada. The wealth of Canada is not equally distributed among the provinces, and immigrants have varying chances of success. Thus, in Quebec the lower wages, in the Prairies the lower land values and a certain lack of business opportunities, render the situation of immigrants less favourable. Highly industrialized Ontario offers undoubtedly the best opportunities for immigrants, and it is no wonder that the bulk of post-war immigration

[2]O. J. Firestone, *Residential Real Estate in Canada* (Toronto, 1951), pp. 98–105.

TABLE III
FINANCIAL STANDING OF 112 HUNGARIAN
IMMIGRANTS, 1952

Class	Number	Percentage
Well-to-do	38	33.9
Medium	53	47.3
Poor	21	18.8
Total	112	100.0

tended toward this province. Furthermore, the importance of the time factor in financial success must not be overlooked. The members of our group have lived for a long time in Canada and their position cannot be compared with that of a recently arrived group. Thus, the sample cannot represent those Hungarians who live in other provinces or who arrived recently in Canada.

The Three Classes

The three financial classes show how successful the immigrants were in achieving their great goal. As a matter of fact, the classes show that within the ethnic group three types of immigrants can be distinguished, types which differ in psychological traits as well as in social status.

The type of the well-to-do immigrant is represented in the tobacco farmer or in urban people who own two or more properties such as two houses or a house and a business. Some of them owned even more. Eleven members owned properties estimated at over $100,000, with $180,000 being the greatest wealth owned by one family. Two life histories will illustrate how immigrants piled up such fortunes.

During the depression, A. could not find steady work, but used to go out to the tobacco country for harvest work. In 1933 he moved out as a share-grower and in the following year he took over a farm with the understanding that he would pay for it as he could. The land, previously used for cattle raising, had to be converted into tobacco land, and A. had no capital. Fortunately, his two sons were old enough to help around, and, except for harvesting, they never used hired labour. The family spent little for food, living on the produce of the farm and buying only such items as salt and spices. "One spring we ran out of potatoes, and it was almost like a sin to buy some for money." Soon, however, the farm began to pay. In 1941, A. exchanged it for a better one, and in 1946 he made another exchange; his present farm was estimated to be worth $100,000. In 1950 he purchased another farm, which is managed by his younger son. He has a house in the small town near to the farm. The house is now rented, but he plans to retire there in a few years. He has a lot on Lake Erie where he once planned to build a cottage. His property was valued at $180,000, and, according to friends, there was a mortgage of about $30,000 on it. Those few years before retirement were regarded as time enough to pay off the mortgage.

The life of B. shows success in urban milieu. At the end of the depression B. was working as a miner and accumulated some savings. In 1940 he returned to Toronto and, although his single status was a serious handicap, he went into business. First, he became partner in a grocery store, then in a lunch bar, and finally in a trucking business. He purchased fruits and vegetables on his own account from farms and sold them to Toronto grocers. Similarly he delivered cattle from the Prairies. He was already regarded as prosperous when he married and acquired a large rooming house in Toronto. After the war he purchased a summer-resort lodge which he still operates. His wealth was estimated at $65,000. According to informants, he is not mortgaged, but on the contrary has savings in the bank.

The life histories of the well-to-do immigrants seem to point to three factors as being instrumental in financial success. In the first place, it seems to be correlated with married status and the support of a "good" sib. All but two well-to-do people were married, whereas the number of bachelors was strikingly high among the poor. Similarly, many strongly knit, well-functioning sibs could be observed among the rich. A. had two well-to-do sib families; B. went into business with his sib people; and in many other cases financial success was greatly helped by a loan advanced by relatives.

An opinion general among the respondents holds that those people prove to be successful who manifest a keen purpose in pursuit of their goals. Such a psychological factor seems, indeed, to be important. All immigrants aimed to make money, but some of them failed in endurance and gave up. Some others were inconsistent in fixing their aims, tried different, often unrealistic schemes, and dabbled in many ways. The purposeful person avoided such pitfalls. A., having found a suitable occupation, stayed in it doggedly. B.'s different business ventures were logical steps in a small but successful business expansion.

Social competition within the ethnic group furnished a drive important to success. Strange as it may sound, the semi-feudal social system of Hungary brought to life a keen competition. The peasants of the villages were constantly vying for social gains. It was regarded as a "virtue" to "outdo" other people of similar standing, and a successful person "bestowed honour" upon his entire sib. This old-country mentality could be easily transplanted into Canadian surroundings, and it worked as a social pressure upon many members of the ethnic group. Thus, when commenting upon somebody who had purchased a cottage, our informant remarked: "Why, he doesn't need it at all. But he could not bear that X. people should have one."

Competition, however, has its own rules in every society. In America, competition centres around monetary goals, and financial success represents the self-realization of the individual. Hungarian society, on the other hand, acknowledged many other than financial goals of competition. Many people withdrew from financial competition and achieved prestige through excellence in some other fields. A penniless count with a gentlemanly behaviour or a poverty-stricken poet with literary achievements often had a greater prestige than a business executive. The effects of such a social system can be easily recognized in the career of the immigrants.

The well-to-do immigrant conceived his goal in financial terms, pursued it purposefully and tried to outdo his countrymen in amassing wealth. Another type of immigrant, however, found other ways of self-realization and was not eager to participate in financial competition. This type is rather common in the medium class of the sample. The life history of a typical member of this class can be summed up in a few sentences:

C. came to Canada in 1924, and from 1928 on, except for some lay-offs during the depression, he was employed by the same factory in Toronto. In 1937 he purchased a home, exchanged it three years later for a rooming house, and after the war he made another property exchange. His property was valued at $18,000, but our informants added that he had money in the bank. He was generally described as very industrious and thrifty; one who withdrew from clubs and social parties, and spent his time tinkering at home, or helping his grown-up children.

Indeed, the medium class, the most numerous in the sample, falls into two categories. Some of its members participate eagerly in the social competition, and soon move upward; a few good years may qualify them for the well-to-do class. These prospective well-to-do's like to keep up with the richer members and are particularly interested in common social affairs such as big parties or reputable clubs where the two classes freely mix. Other members of the medium class seem to be more or less satisfied with their present state and apparently do not long for any conspicuous upward move. They have the feeling that they have taken care of their old age, and they do not intend to participate in group competition. As outlets for their self-realization, they are interested in many hobbies popular in Canada or Hungary. They like the weekly card parties where they discuss politics, tell jokes and even folktales. They like fishing, write poetry, participate in church activities, and devote much time to their families. Anyone who wishes to find the happy immigrant should look around in their circle.

The poor class of the sample included both real have-nots and families owning well cared-for homes. However, the outstanding feature of the class was that it could be divided into four families each possessing a home valued at over $10,000, and seventeen bachelors who did not own any property. The poor class, in the strict sense of the word, can be described as the class of the bachelors. The term "bachelor," as used in our study, denotes all those persons who lived as single men in Canada, although some of them had a family in the old country.

Table IV seems to corroborate the common saying of immigrants that bachelors "make no good." Although not all of them are poor, and one bachelor of the "poor" class was said to have $14,000 in the bank, the bachelors seem to lack the drive to accumulate wealth in real estate. Their poor showing is partly due to the fact that the financial success of immigrants is correlated with marital status. New immigrant groups, including the Hungarians, are characterized by an excess of males over females. Hence, a poor man finds it hard to

TABLE IV

BACHELORS IN A GROUP OF
112 HUNGARIAN IMMIGRANTS

Class	Number	Percentage of the class
Well-to-do	2	5.3
Medium	3	5.7
Poor	17	81.0
Total	22	19.6

get a wife. Furthermore, marriage itself is a great help in improving financial position. The wife represents a second wage earner, whereas the expenditures of a married couple are scarcely more than those of bachelor life. Married people have better opportunities of advancement in their jobs, and single men cannot go into businesses which are, on this level, all family operated.

The mores of the Hungarian group further affect the same point. It is a postulate of the in-group competition that every family "must show" something. If a family does not make good, it is regarded as a failure. There were families who failed; they "had no face" before the community; they severed the ties and moved away where no Hungarians lived. The same social pressure, however, does not apply to bachelors. The bachelor has been a common type in all classes of Hungary, and was allowed greater freedom in sexual matters and in the financial field than a married man. Therefore a bachelor is not ostracized because he has remained poor, but is accepted by the immigrant group as a member in good standing. His social status is determined by his sib, and a poor bachelor from a well-to-do sib may share the social life of the well-to-do class.

Two life histories will illuminate the plight of single men of the poor class.

D. had a well-paid, but seasonal occupation as bricklayer where he would work eight to nine months a year. He saved during this time, and in winter lived on his savings and unemployment insurance. In the last weeks before spring he was often compelled to borrow a few dollars from relatives. His friends described him as "quarrelsome." Several times he had to leave his job because of some quarrel with the foreman or his fellow workers. For many years he used to be a member of a Hungarian club, but was finally asked to leave the premises. When meeting other Hungarians, he was soon engaged in some political discussion, defending his principles in an aggressive way and resenting contradictions. He liked to visit his sib people, and a woman among them commented on him: "Joe is indeed a hard fellow. Whenever he is here, I wish he did not come. But after all, he is a relative and one must care for her relatives."

E. was apparently slow in movement and speech and, in the judgment of other Hungarians, "not too bright." His life was full of failures. Married in Hungary, he left his wife with one child behind when emigrating. She later bore another child, and this fact would perhaps explain why E. never "brought her out." His life in Canada was an endless series of short jobs, both in farming and industry, none lasting more than a year. He never liked the city, and for the last sixteen years he has worked in the tobacco country. He would work from spring to late fall, but in winter he "took it easy." In a good year he would spend a few weeks in Toronto; in a poor one, he took a winter job, or lived on the credit of his grocer, landlady or old acquaintances. The only stable feature of his life in Canada has been his attachment to a Hungarian widow of some means whom he has visited for many years. Actually, he wanted to marry her and intended to get a divorce in Hungary. The plan was rejected by the widow, apparently because of E.'s poverty.

The life of the poor immigrants is characterized by instability. Their occupational instability is mirrored by their preference for seasonal work, their instability in human relations, their bachelor status. Their behaviour indicates some personality maladjustment. During their first years in Canada, however, most immigrants manifest various signs of maladjustment. It seems that those persons who overcome the initial stage of maladjustment within a reasonable time become successful, while those who are unable to find their place in Canada and to make a good occupational adjustment stay poor and single. Our sample, and perhaps all immigrant groups, contain both successful and maladjusted people. Altogether it is very likely that both types are more common in an emigrant population than in the total population of the country of emigration.

The members of the sample came from the same social class in Hungary and arrived without any money. They became differentiated during the years in Canada while their present wealth was being built up. The process of becoming prosperous is illuminated by Chart 2, which shows the number of properties acquired by the immigrants in each year from 1930 to 1952.[3] As it can be seen, in the decade prior to 1940 less than ten properties were acquired in each year. In other words, the Hungarian group in Ontario was homogeneous, poor, hard pressed by the crisis, drudging in temporary jobs, hit by unemployment and lacking savings. Under such circumstances only a few immigrants could manage to acquire property. The situation changed with the war boom. Immigrants obtained well-paid, steady jobs where they worked and saved. At the earliest moment they converted their savings into real estate; and from 1940 on, they represented a significant buying group on the real estate market.[4] After an unusually high number of property acquisitions in the years 1945 to 1947, a saturation point was reached, and the buying declined relatively.

Although the great majority of the group has been living in Canada for a considerable time, only the last fifteen years, the period of boom, were decisive in acquiring wealth. It was not until this period that the types of well-to-do and poor immigrants differentiated, and that a social stratification within the group was established. The years of social disorganization which characterize the first phase of every immigrant group were prolonged by the economic crisis, but after 1940 the Hungarian group moved fast toward a stable social integration.

Ways to Riches

The immigrant landing in Canada knew neither the country nor the language. He possessed nothing except his unskilled labour. That could be sold, but even labour sells poorly in its raw form. Actually, every

[3]The curve of real estate acquisitions by Hungarians shows a certain similarity to the curve of real estate transfers in the Province of Ontario (Firestone, *Residential Real Estate*, p. 147). The main difference is that the Hungarian curve shows a decline after 1946, whereas the Ontario curve rises to 1949, the last year of the table.

[4]John Kosa, "Hungarian Immigrants in North America: Their Ecology and Residential Mobility," *Canadian Journal of Economics and Political Science*, XXII (Aug. 1956).

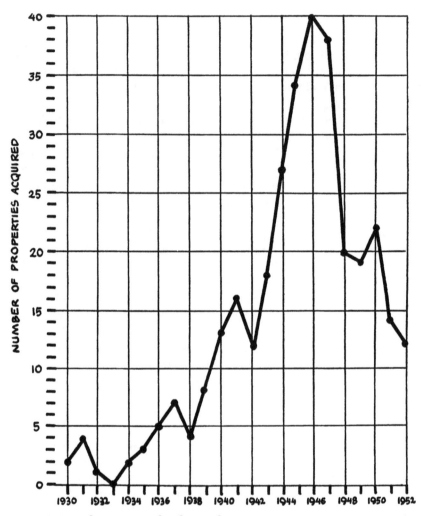

CHART 2. Annual acquisition of real estate by 112 Hungarian immigrants, 1930–52.

immigrant had to make an occupational adjustment in his new country.[5] The former farmhand from Hungary had to re-learn farming under Canadian conditions; other people acquired skills and trades here and became bricklayers, carpenters, or plumbers; the whole group had to find out what business opportunities lend themselves to immigrants. It took them a long time to find their place in the occupational

[5]Erdmann D. Beynon, "Occupational Succession of Hungarians in Detroit," *American Journal of Sociology*, XXXIX (March 1934).

stratification of the new country. But once the occupational adjustment was achieved, the ways to riches opened up.

Among the many ways that lead to wealth, speculation can be ruled out offhand. Speculation needs more knowledge than these immigrants had. Although the phantasy of newcomers plays with speculative schemes, few of them will be able to realize those plans. A few Hungarians own stocks as investment; a few of them buy lots in the hope of their values rising; a gold prospecting party of Hungarians went up north and returned half-starved and with smashed hopes; a Hungarian spinster struck it rich when the late Sir Harry Oakes prospected gold on her property at Kirkland Lake.[6] Altogether, such business ventures did not contribute essentially to the wealth of the Hungarian group.

Business, on the other hand, gave fair chances to make money. There are few well-to-do or medium class immigrants who have not tried their luck in some business or other, particularly in the three popular ones, rooming house, lunch bar, and grocery store.

The rooming-house business is actually a part-time job. The members of the family may have other full-time jobs and discharge the duties around the house in their spare time. Moreover, children of the family may be well used in the different chores. Thus, the rooming house is lucrative because it utilizes almost completely the family's spare-time labour. Similar is the case with lunch bars, grocery stores, plumbing or gardening. Apparently Hungarians participate in all those fields of business that are open to people with small capital and an imperfect knowledge of English. They prefer family-operated businesses and avoid employing outside help.

Farming was the occupation which contributed the lion's share to the wealth of the Hungarians. Every member of the group has been engaged at some time in agriculture, and the richest ones, all with property worth more than $100,000, were farmers. The great majority of Hungarians came from a rural background. In Hungary, however, the agricultural knowledge of poor peasants, the stratum which gave us our immigrants, was regarded as unsatisfactory. The "dwarf farms" were run uneconomically, and the agricultural labourers carried out the orders of their masters and never had an opportunity to acquire an adequate knowledge of farm management.[7]

---

[6]Jenö Ruzsa, A kanadai margyarság története (Toronto, 1940), pp. 91–2, 228–30.

[7]Mihály Kerék, A magyar földkérdés (Budapest, 1939); P. T. Bauer and John Kosa, Az európai parasztság jövője (Budapest, 1937).

The average Hungarian who landed in Canada, however, though he was no expert farm operator, had certain ideas and principles. He knew that marketing could replace self-sufficiency; he was aware of the importance of improvements, of mechanization, of competition. In Hungary he had not had a chance to apply such principles, but in Canada his theoretical knowledge, matched with a strong drive to get along, worked well. The history of the tobacco growers in the counties of Norfolk, Oxford and Elgin in the Province of Ontario demonstrates their success.

In the estimate of the local Hungarian priest, there were about three thousand tobacco farms in that part of the province. About one thousand of them, those of top quality, belonged to Belgians, about a thousand to Hungarians, and the remainder were owned by Slovaks, Germans, Poles, Lithuanians and Canadians. Thirty years earlier the same district with its sandy soil had been an impoverished part of Ontario. Then in about 1925 Belgian immigrants established the first tobacco farms. Soon Hungarians were coming up from Hamilton and Toronto as temporary workers, the first Hungarian settling in Delhi, one of the local centres, in 1929. Since tobacco proved to be profitable during the depression, these years of crisis attracted many people. New Hungarian settlers came from a wider and wider circle, from the northern mining district, from Quebec, and finally even from the West where farming suffered much under the crisis.[8] The prices of farms were low, and with two years' savings as a miner, sometimes with a down payment as low as $100, one could acquire farmland.

The transformation of pasture or grain field into tobacco farm was the great proving ground for newcomers. Besides strenuous labour, it required capital which none of the Hungarian settlers possessed. However, with small loans and by investing the first year's returns they got along somehow. According to a local informer, none of the Hungarians in the area failed except those who did not go into farming. The boom of the war years came as a great help. At the end of the war, "there were no more Hungarian sharegrowers" in the counties. All of them had succeeded in buying their farms. The early settlers paid off their mortgages and bought a second farm; some older people leased out

[8]The Hungarian population of the three counties increased as follows:

County	1921	1931	1941	1951
Elgin	10	126	544	1121
Norfolk	8	153	1308	2089
Oxford	–	99	493	788
Total	18	378	2345	3998

their property and retired into the small towns of the tobacco country. Their success became proverbial among Hungarians, and the district attracted many newcomers. At the time of our research, a well-to-do Hungarian community, divided into different occupational and financial strata, was living there.

Farming and business rewarded the immigrant with a good income, but his financial success was rooted in saving. Every immigrant knew at the time of his arrival that he must save in order to get ahead. A common piece of advice given to newcomers is to stay in a steady job and spend every week somewhat less than the pay. Moreover, it is an old observation that minority groups may live more thriftily because they are not bound by those status requirements which are so important in the spending habits of the majority. Those ethnic groups which played a prominent role in early capitalism (Jews, Armenians, Greeks, Huguenots) were able to save and amass wealth because they were not encumbered by those expenses that a nobleman or burgher had to shoulder in order to maintain his status. The budget of the Hungarian immigrant family reveals a similar situation.

Among the expenditures for necessities of life, the rent is of special interest because of its bearing upon the ecology of American cities. When Hungarians began to settle in Toronto about 1930, the economic crisis was already being felt. They took up residence in a deteriorated, low-rent area closed in by Beverley Street and Spadina Avenue and by Queen and College. They lived there under extremely poor housing conditions. A family often had to be satisfied with one room, or two families shared a three-room flat; in other cases a number of roomers were taken in.

Although the housing conditions of their class in Hungary were extremely poor, the immigrants wished something better in Canada and hated the slum in Toronto. They did not stay there because it reminded them of similar slums in the old country, or because they had no higher pretensions. On the contrary, they found the dilapidated buildings, dirty streets, and lack of sanitary facilities "abominable." They had a strong dislike of the other inhabitants of the slum, immigrants of other nationalities. They complained about the bad environment the area offered their children. Such complaints as follow were typical: "Children grow up there as bums," "The house was good enough for Negroes or Jews, but not for people like us," "I loathed it [the slum] day and night, but we had to bear it."

The immigrant moved into a slum because he could not afford better housing. However, when the economic situation improved, when income became regular and saving possible, he stayed there for a while in order to save on rent. When he saved enough to buy his home, he left the slum for good. He selected a "nice" home on a "good" street with "decent" neighbours; one family was very proud of the fact that its neighbour was a manager of a large public-utility company. About the end of the war, the Hungarian island in the Beverley area disappeared. The immigrants acquired homes and dispersed over the metropolitan area of Toronto.

Food is an item of the family budget where good housewives can prove their thrift. In the Hungarian peasant community, as in every other community, certain customs regulated the use of food. Thus, "it was a shame" if a woman did not keep a good kitchen or did not show hospitality to a visitor. On the other hand, it was a virtue to utilize all left-overs. To cast away bread or milk or let anything be spoiled was considered squandering. Such customs could well be reconciled with the daily life in Canada, and the women did their best to save in the kitchen. Once a week they would visit the market where prices were cheaper; they baked cakes and regarded it as a sin to buy them; in summer they preserved fruits and vegetables; in winter the family bought a whole pig and sacks of potatoes direct from the farm. Altogether the food as well as the housing shows that immigrants are willing to give up comfort and popular luxuries of American life for saving's sake.

Saving on necessities of life is limited by the nature of the goods. A great part of the Canadian family's budget is disbursed for items which are not necessities, but give social status. The motor car, a conspicuous expenditure, has beyond its economic utility an outspoken status-giving significance; the acquisition of a late-model car when the old one is not yet worn out is usually prompted by such considerations. The immigrant who renounced luxury or comfort for saving was not willing to undergo financial sacrifices in order to gain status in the Canadian community. Thus, he regarded the car as an economic utility only; he postponed buying one, or satisfied himself with an old one, where a Canadian with similar income would have used a more expensive model. A well-to-do Hungarian, who was working as a part-time salesman also, drove a 12-year-old car and commented thus: "It's good enough for me. Why, I don't want to pick up girls on the street corner."

Clothing, and particularly women's fashions, is another important expenditure in securing social status. Since the immigrant does not participate in the Canadian competition for status, he can save on such items. Moreover, the ideal wife, as conceived by the Hungarian peasant community, is supposed to produce a part of the family's clothing at home, to keep it in good shape by mending and patching and not to cast away any piece that can be still used. Immigrant women do not follow the seasonal changes of fashion, do not buy a new dress for every season and discard it when it goes out of fashion. Although the children "must keep up with their breed" and the Hungarian daughters follow the fashion trends as do other Canadian girls, the average immigrant family saves much on clothing; the women's part in saving must not be underestimated.

The immigrant shows a conscious effort to save on every item of the budget, and the members of the family whole-heartedly co-operate in the saving plan. Saving, however, does not go on without limit. When a certain goal is reached—a house acquired, a part of the mortgage paid off—a psychological saturation point is reached. The rigour of saving is from now on gradually loosened; the family wants "to take it easy," to "enjoy the amenities of life," "to afford what we can." The children should have everything their schoolmates have; the wife should enjoy an easier life with a new range or washing machine; the man should have his share in social affairs. As one informant put it: "When a man is smoking a ten-cent cigar, you may see that he has established himself." From this time on the spending habits of the Hungarian family tend to approach those of Canadian families of similar income and status. The well-to-do people show a conspicuous consumption of cars, household appliances and other semi-durable goods, much the same as Canadian families of similar standing do. At formal parties they follow the Hungarian patterns of conspicuous waste, for example, by breaking the glasses after a drink.

The financial success achieved in Canada has had some lasting effects not only upon the social status of the immigrant, but also upon his personality. His wealth and standard of living have reached those of the lower-middle or middle class in Hungary. In his attitude he is no longer the same down-trodden peasant he used to be in the old country; he has gained self-confidence and self-respect. He is no longer willing to subject himself to the unquestioned leadership of those who come from the Hungarian ruling class; he behaves himself as the equal of any other Hungarian. This "haughtiness" of the former peasant surprised those upper-class immigrants who arrived after 1945, and the émigré press complained about it repeatedly.

A similar change took place in the immigrants' attitude toward Canada. At the time of their arrival, they were prone to disapprove of everything that differed from the old-country pattern. With success accompanying their efforts, they began to approve of and adopt many Canadian traits. Canada ceased to be the country of strange customs, and became a home for life. The main aspect of the new home is not cultural or social, since the immigrant is unable to participate in the Canadian cultural and social life. For him, Canada is, first of all, the country which gives a fair chance for success.

Social Stratification

The members of each social class in Canada or the United States are rather conscious of those differences in income, wealth, and prestige which separate them from other classes. At the same time, however, they acknowledge a general American creed according to which all people in the country should be regarded as equal. This seemingly contradictory situation is dissolved in a working compromise which eliminates the conspicuous manifestations of class differences in many fields of life. Great social mobility renders elastic the boundaries between classes, and, in compliance with the general creed, the great majority of Americans disregard real class differences and share the same form of life.

In those European societies where remnants of feudalism survive, the creed of general equality has never prevailed. Up to recent times no great social mobility has disturbed the stratification as it developed during a long historical process. Status and class are not accessories that can be put aside easily, but are constant traits of the personality which determine the individual's behaviour. Class position manifests itself in every action, and is revealed in the whole form of life. Such a system, as it existed in Hungary up to 1944, was rigid and unjust, but strong and stable. The immigrant, who had been the perennial underdog in the system, wanted to shake it off upon landing in Canada; he wanted not only the easy money, but the blessings of the Canadian system of social stratification as well. However, the ties of the Hungarian system were too strong to be put aside by a simple change of country. As a result, a particular social stratification has been built up by the Hungarian group in Canada which mingles both Hungarian and Canadian traits.

At the time of their arrival the immigrants were, indeed, equal— equal in poverty. But success in Canada broke down the original equality and developed differences. The wealth acquired by the group is unequally distributed among the classes (see Table V). One-third of the group, the well-to-do, owned two-thirds of the total assets; on the other hand, one-fifth of the group shared in only one-sixtieth of the assets. Such an unequal distribution of wealth means, in our society, a class system. The small group of 112 families is clearly divided into three classes which roughly coincide with the financial classification.

TABLE V

VALUE OF PROPERTIES OWNED BY
112 HUNGARIAN IMMIGRANTS (BY CLASSES)

Class	Members		Total value of properties	
	No.	%	$	%
Well-to-do	38	33.9	2,306,000	65.4
Medium	53	47.3	1,166,000	33.1
Poor	21	18.8	54,000	1.5
Total	112	100.0	3,526,000	100.0

Class position involves not only the possession of wealth, but also a commensurate prestige. Well-to-do people with their prestige look down upon the poor, while the poor are supposed to demonstrate a certain reverence towards their well-to-do countrymen. But at the same time, the sample group claims to acknowledge the American creed of the basic equality of men.[9] Thus, a contradiction similar to the American contradiction exists between the real situation and the claimed postulate. The Hungarian immigrants, however, resolved this contradiction in a way divergent from the American solution, and the result was a certain animosity or even hostility between the classes. Well-to-do people often refer to the poor as lazy, no-good, and easy-going; the latter describe the rich as haughty, dominant, and money-hungry. The medium class, because of its special position, is relatively free from social resentment, but some of them scoff at persons both above and below their own class.[10]

The group is conscious of the existing class articulation, and one member often describes another as "not our kind." The social cliques usually include families "of the same kind." At six formal parties given

[9]The new immigrants coming from the upper classes do not seem to acknowledge the postulate of equality. Thus, refugees living in Europe and America published a new volume of the Yearbook of Hungarian Nobility as late as 1953.

[10]In the Hungarian community of Detroit it was found that the successful people develop hostile attitudes towards lower-class Hungarians and attempt to gain acceptance among native status groups (Erdmann D. Beynon, "Social Mobility and Social Distance among Hungarian Immigrants in Detroit," American Journal of Sociology, XLI, Jan. 1936).

by well-to-do families we noted the names of the guests and tried to place them according to their class. It was found that two-thirds of the guests could be placed in the well-to-do class, the remainder in the medium class. The only guest from the poor class was a sib man of one host. Within the sib everybody is equal, and class differentiation can be applied only to people outside the sib; there it is a pre-eminent point in choosing one's friends. Well-to-do people stick together and accept as equals only some "thriving" families of the medium class who are on their way to become well-to-do. The poor, left out of other groupings, must keep to themselves.

The relation of G. and H. illustrates how class differences work out in every-day life. G. and H. were of the same village and of the same age, had been friends since the first school days, came almost at the same time to Canada. Here G. became a well-to-do farmer, whereas H., a bachelor, remained a poor agricultural worker. The old friendship ties, however, have never been renounced. H. may visit G.'s home at any time, and he does so quite often. In need he gets small loans and presents such as old clothing. Every Christmas Day he is asked for dinner, but when family G. gives a formal party on Boxing Day, H. is not invited. If H. drops in, he is seated in the kitchen, whereas the guests of equal class are invited into the living room. On account of the old friendship, H. addresses Mr. and Mrs. G. in intimate forms which involve social equality; but when speaking to the grown-up children of the family, he uses those forms of the Hungarian which are for people of higher status. In other words, the old friendship is maintained, but it is not the friendship of the social clique; it is tinted with class differences.

The etiquette which characterizes the relation between G. and H., and which reminds one of the race relations in the Deep South, was the common rule in the Hungarian village community. Social intercourse among the different strata of the peasantry was regulated by an elaborate code of etiquette which aimed at expressing the social distance between the parties. The mutual observance of that etiquette, as with the etiquette of race relations, did not obscure the fact that the classes were separated by sharp cleavages. The time-honoured etiquette was not a denial, but an acknowledgment of class antitheses.[11]

The sharp social differentiation of the Hungarian group in Canada has been developed during the last fifteen years when the immigrants

[11]Concerning etiquette as the formal expression of social distance, see Manó Kertész, Szállok az urnak (Budapest, 1932); Viola Tomory, A parasztság szemlélete (Budapest, 1935).

made money. A period of fifteen years seems to be short to build up an intricate social system, but the Hungarians brought from the old country certain patterns of class structure; and when they struck it rich in Canada, these patterns flourished. Wealth, which is the basis for this class differentiation, is determined by the Canadian economic situation; but the manifestations of the class system, such as etiquette, can be traced to its sources in Hungary.

The sample group mirrors only the social stratification of those immigrants who came from the poor classes of Hungary. Prior to 1940, the number of Hungarians from higher classes was small, an estimated 5 to 7 per cent of the Hungarians in Canada. With post-war immigration their number multiplied, and now it is estimated at over 10,000, that is, one-sixth or one-fifth of the total Hungarian group. They came from the lower middle, middle, and ruling classes of Hungary, and show a sharp cleavage from one another and particularly from the poor classes. The fate of the immigrant in Canada differs according to his class origin.

The members of the former ruling class came without the wealth necessary to maintain their former status, but with ranks and titles originating in a social and political system that had collapsed at the end of World War II. They never surrendered their ranks and titles and theoretically nobody can bestow them upon other persons. They cling to the titles, even if the title claimed is in sharp contrast with their real status in Canada. Thus, a Hungarian paper reported on a political meeting where the speaker was "His Dignity, Noble, Valiant, Dr. X.Y., Hungarian Royal Colonel, Member of Parliament, National President of the World Federation for Hungarian Reconstruction," but revealed in another issue that the gentleman was working as a labourer in Canada. Another meeting had as chairman "His Excellency, General of the Army Y.Z.," a man who was making a living as night watchman. Sometimes titles turn out to be lucrative in Canada, as in the case of a Hungarian count who was helped into a better job by some newspaper publicity; but the titled class as a whole is somewhat slow to make a good occupational adjustment after immigration. However, they try to maintain prestige through exclusiveness, displayed in an esoteric social life. No lower-class people are admitted to their Sunday afternoon parties given in a back room of a rooming house where the old titles are strictly maintained and the guests address one another as "My Dignified Ladyship" or "My Excellent Lord and Dear Brother."

Immigrants of middle-class origin brought along less conspicuous titles which could be dropped unnoticed on Canadian soil. On the other hand, they had a good education, many of them a working knowledge of English, some professional skill or business experience, a certain capital or at least money enough to bridge the first period in Canada. With such assets they had a fairly propitious start and succeeded within a short time in acquiring a status comparable to the Canadian white-collar or middle class. For a doctor or engineer the adjustment was obviously easy; the former businessman succeeded fast in establishing his small but independent undertaking; some others secured white-collar jobs such as accountancy—an occupation as much favoured by middle-class people as rooming house business by old immigrants. None of them went into manual labour or into any other occupation that, in the concepts of the old Hungarian system, is incompatible with middle-class status.

The lower-middle class, the petty *bourgeoisie*, was a special formation of some European societies which, actually, had no counterpart in the American social system. It was separated by a wide cleavage from the higher classes; on the other hand, it claimed a superiority over the poor classes and possessed certain privileges; for example, the subaltern positions in the civil service were their exclusive bailiwick. Deprived of the old privileges, the lower-middle class immigrants could not find a stable point of orientation in Canada. Their social prejudices caused them to despise the factory worker's life; a lack of capital and education barred them from white-collar occupations. Such an unfortunate start was hard to overcome in the short period after their arrival, and the group shows many signs of disorganization and maladjustment. Unable to find their place in Canadian society, they are waiting for a political change in Hungary and plan to return there. With such an attitude they may approach the former ruling class, approach it not in its social exclusiveness, but in those *émigré* political organizations which have sprung up since the war. The political organizations of Hungarian *émigrés* are actually led by members of the former ruling class, but their membership is recruited from the lower-middle class who are willing to accept the duties of the rank and file.[12]

Immigration and life in Canada did not bring together the Hungarian upper and lower classes. The rhythm of immigration reinforced the class differences. Old immigrants from the lower class became rich

---

[12]Concerning similar observations among the Czechoslovaks see Jiri Kolaja, "A Sociological Note on the Czechoslovak Anti-Communist Refugee," *American Journal of Sociology*, LVIII (Nov. 1952).

in Canada, while the new ones from the upper class have lost their wealth through war and Communism. The usual animosity which exists within ethnic groups between oldtimers and newcomers is particularly accentuated among Hungarians. The old immigrant has the feeling that the new ones received more and undeserved support in immigration and explains it in terms of the old social injustices. The Hungarian saying: "A lord is a lord even in hell" was travestied with political sarcasm: "A lord is a lord even in democracy." The upper classes, on the other hand, resent the lack of reverence among lower-class Hungarians and object that former peasants now want to be on an equal level with their former masters.

None of the classes sees any good reason to alter its old policies. The lower and upper classes are sealed off even more hermetically than was the case in Hungary. This class antagonism atomizes the Hungarian group and blocks the way to common action. Hungarian clubs and organizations, to some extent even churches, seem to identify themselves with one of the classes and do not receive co-operation from other classes. Those persons who are dissatisfied with the social system of the group, peculiar and cumbersome in the Canadian environment, cannot change it, but may withdraw from the group—and a few have done so.

Old immigrants base their class system on the reality of wealth; new immigrants, on claims rooted in the past political system. Reality and claims cannot be interchanged; the classes of the Hungarian group do not make up a continuous ladder where a successful individual could step up to the highest rungs. The stratification, as depicted in Chart 3, shows two independent pyramids. They are not linked with the normal channels of ascent which characterize every lively, sound society. Such a situation cannot be reconciled with the Canadian class system, for the Hungarian classes of new immigrants are not horizontal with the Canadian class boundaries. This fact is represented by the slanting borderlines of the new immigrants' pyramid showing that, for example, members of the former Hungarian ruling class are now dispersed among various Canadian classes.[13]

This strange and complicated Hungarian class system cannot be maintained in the face of Canadian society. American society is unaware of, and does not acknowledge, the internal status system of minority groups. A sleeping-car porter was at one time regarded as a

[13]A similar social division was observed among the Russian immigrants by Frances L. Reinhold, "Exiles and Refugees in American History," *Annals of the American Academy of Political and Social Science*, CCIII (May 1939).

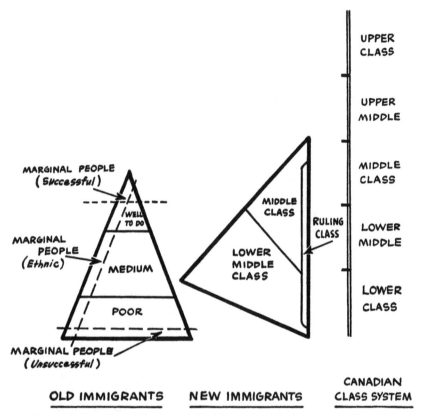

CHART 3. Social stratification of the Hungarian ethnic group in Canada.

middle-class person by the Negro group, but not by American society. Similarly, American society ranks the members of minority groups according to general American principles. They are ranked on the basis of some objective traits such as occupation, income, etc., and of the subjective valuation concomitant with their membership in a minority group. The Hungarian immigrant doctor, for example, is accepted as a professional and placed in the corresponding Canadian class. However, he lives, or has his office, in an ethnic island of the city, and draws his patients and selects his friends mostly out of the ethnic group. As a result, his status in the Canadian system is a shade lower than that of the average native-born doctor. Hungarian farmers represent a considerable portion of the wealth in the tobacco country, but they, as well as other immigrants, furnish only a small share of the social news in the local papers. Their names are hardly known and do not arouse great interest in the native-born community. In other words, their status is somewhat lower than that of Canadian farmers with similar possessions.

Every member of the ethnic group has, as a matter of fact, two social statuses, one within the group and another one in Canadian society. The two ratings, except in few cases, do not coincide.[14] The social discrepancy is sometimes conspicuous indeed, as in the case of unsuccessful bachelors or former generals turned labourers. In every case, however, the in-group status is higher and more coveted. Indeed, the status-giving authority of the ethnic group is an important associative force; a great number of immigrants are strongly attached to their group because there they find a higher status, greater self-respect, and more security than Canadian society allots them. Only those people leave the ethnic group by their own will who have already acquired a satisfactory status and security in the Canadian system.

The status system of the group is the main incentive of in-group competition. The Hungarian values connected with social stratification differed considerably from the Canadian ones, and the Hungarians had more reason to rely upon the status given by the group. The consideration of individual and sib prestige enforced the form of life set up by the ethnic community. Thus, none of the maladjusted persons became criminal because the same in-group system protected them with a certain status and security.

The Hungarian ethnic group, although small, shows a social structure more complex than a Canadian group of similar size, because it has been shaped by both the Canadian and the Hungarian value systems of social stratification. The impact of the Canadian system, as shown by the old immigrants, developed within fifteen years a class structure which is somewhat similar to that of a Canadian small town. The behaviour of new immigrants indicates that the old country's social system, when supported by self-interest, is obstinate in its survival and willing to defy Canadian reality. The striking antithesis between the two social systems will very likely diminish in the future, but it will not disappear. The immigrant will always live in a strange mixture of two disparate social structures. An ethnic group, however small, will always reveal the social system of the old country as a drop of sea water reveals the secrets of far deep seas.

[14]Ethnic groups in the United States had lower prestige scores on the average than did the old Yankee stock in the same community. See Elin L. Anderson, *We Americans* (Cambridge, Mass., 1938); W. Lloyd Warner and Leo Srole, *The Social Systems of American Ethnic Groups* (New Haven, 1945); Harold E. Kaufman, *Prestige Classes in a New York Rural Community* (Cornell Agricultural Experiment Station, Memoir 260, Ithaca, 1943).

CHAPTER IV

MARRIAGE AND FAMILY

WORK AND SAVING are governed by rational considerations. They reveal the reasoning personality which is prone to make calculated adjustments in order to achieve a set goal. The immigrant is willing to adjust himself to the requirements of the country of choice in order to achieve success. Marriage and family life, on the other hand, are necessarily tied up with basic human drives and emotions which, by their nature, limit rational considerations. The adjustment made in this field will disclose those steps of the assimilation process which are non-rational and non-conscious. A study of the family life of the Hungarian group will show how the old-country and new-country patterns clash and how a compromise between them is worked out.

Selecting a Mate

When the immigrant gains access to the "easy" money in Canada, he has to renounce many amenities of life. The strange, new environment, the lack of personal connections, his timidity or bewilderment force him to lead a life which can be called in many respects unnatural. Thus, he does not find in the new country a "normal" marriage market where he could select his mate and establish his family in the "usual" way; in addition to the various financial difficulties, he is confronted with another hard problem, that of getting a wife.

As shown in Table VI, less than half of the sample group were married at the time of immigration. Some of the married people arrived with wife and children, and experienced from the first moment all the joys and worries of married life. Others left a wife behind; they planned to work and save, and send for the family. In their case, normal family life was interrupted, sometimes for many years. One Hungarian farmer spent twenty-two years separated from his wife, and she joined him only after World War II. A long separation may lead to a permanent disruption of the family life. Some immigrants, indeed, have never been joined by their families, others obtained a divorce in Hungary and remarried in Canada. Only four persons stated that "they have a family" in the old country, but, considering all the facts known

TABLE VI

MARITAL ARRANGEMENT OF 112 HUNGARIAN IMMIGRANT MEN

	No.	%
Married before immigration		
Immigrated with wife	17	15.2
Was followed by wife	26	23.2
Has been separated through immigration	6*	5.3
Total	49	43.7
Married after immigration		
Was engaged at the time of immigration and was followed by bride	15	13.4
Engaged and married during stay in Canada	32	28.6
Total	47	42.0
Single†	16	14.3
Total	112	100.0

*Estimated figure.
†The single and separated group of this table make up the "bachelor" group described in chapter III.

to us, we denoted six persons in the group as having been separated but not divorced. It is very likely that separation and divorce show higher rates among immigrants than in the total population. Separation through immigration loosens the family ties,[1] and an unhappy marriage might prompt men to leave the old country. In some cases, undoubtedly, emigration was tantamount to desertion.[2]

The majority of the sample were not married at the time of immigration. Some of them were engaged, and when they saved enough they sent for the girl and realized their marriage plan. Nevertheless, it is estimated that over 40 per cent of the group was unable to establish a normal family life within a reasonable time after immigration because special difficulties faced immigrants in contracting marriage. The establishment of a family was, first of all, a matter of finances. The groom had to pay the cost of immigration for his bride, and thus the financial prerequisites of marriage were burdensome. The great depression wrecked many marriage plans and when the economic situation improved, war stopped immigration from Hungary. The

[1]See *Report on Counselling and Orientation Service of Canadian Citizenship Council in Aurich, Germany,* published in mimeographed form by the Canadian Citizenship Council, Ottawa.
[2]In the 1920's it was estimated that 18,000 Russian and Polish Jews had deserted their wives in the old country and migrated to America. Louis Wirth, *The Ghetto* (Chicago, 1928), p. 216.

Hungarians in Canada were blocked in getting mates from the old country; at the same time, they were confronted with a lack of eligible females in Canada.

The Hungarians, like other recently immigrated groups, showed a surplus of males over females (see Table VII). Over the last decades, the excess of males has varied according to two main factors: the immigration which usually brings in a surplus of males, and the natural increase of the ethnic group where the distribution of sexes is normal. In periods with heavy immigration, the ethnic group shows a great surplus of males; in periods when natural increase is more important than increase through immigration, the ethnic group tends to approach the normal distribution of sexes.

TABLE VII

DISTRIBUTION OF SEXES, POPULATION OF HUNGARIAN ORIGIN IN CANADA, 1921–51

Year	Number of males per 1,000 females
1921	1,112
1931	1,615
1941	1,273
1951	1,197

In 1921 the rate of sexes was at the nearest point to the normal, and the situation may be rightly attributed to the seven-year interruption of Hungarian immigration caused by the war. After 1925 a new great wave of immigration appeared, and the 1931 census showed the highest surplus of males. Depression and war again halted immigration, and in 1941 the distribution of sexes approached the normal state. The situation was similar even during the decade from 1941 to 1951, for although a considerable number of Hungarian immigrants arrived after 1947, the Canadian immigration policy opened the country to many single female D.P.'s; furthermore, the distribution of sexes was more equal among the new, higher-class immigrants than among the old ones. In old times, the poor men came alone, whereas the new immigrants from the better-off classes arrived with their families.

In the immigrant group, if considered separately from the total population of Hungarian origin, the shortage of females was even worse. In 1931, the adult immigrant group showed 219 males for every 100 females, and the ratio of eligible males to eligible females was 3.27, the second highest rate among the ethnic groups of the census.[3] The uneven geographical distribution of the sexes added to the difficulties. Relatively more Hungarian girls could be found in the Prairie Provinces or in the United States where the old immigrants had settled than in eastern Canada where the newcomers gathered.[4]

Intermarriage is usually difficult for a new immigrant group, and particularly so for the Hungarians with their lingual and national peculiarities. Italian and French, Polish and Ukrainian intermarriages do not present serious difficulties, but the Hungarians, having no kindred peoples, maintained a certain endogamy. At the time of the 1931 census, nine out of ten marriages were within the group.[5] The immigrants, as distinct from the Canadian-born of Hungarian origin, show an even lower rate of intermarriage; the sample group, for example, did not include any case of intermarriage. On the other hand, the new immigrants who came after 1945 show a tendency to marry into the Anglo-Canadian stock.

The immigrants of our sample were forced to look to the old country and to find their mates there. Economic crisis and war deferred many marriages, but, after all, those people succeeded in getting a wife who were financially successful, had good sib relations, and displayed purposefulness of action. Pecuniary considerations play, in our society, an important part in marital selection. Financial success rendered the immigrant desirable to the girls in the home village, and many poor girls in Hungary were attracted by the idea of marrying a rich Hungarian overseas. One poor bachelor commented sarcastically upon the marriage of a certain girl, "she married $40,000." Good relations with the sib helped in another respect. Relatives functioned as go-betweens and matchmakers. Their role in "bringing together youthful hearts" was important even in the old Hungarian village community where the customary ways of courtship stood open to the youths. Their help became particularly valuable for the immigrant. Go-betweens could awake a girl's interest in a boy far-away, they could iron out many difficulties, they could persuade a girl to emigrate.[6]

Relatives did not restrict the free choice of the marrying youths.

[3]W. Burton Hurd, "Racial Origins and Nativity of the Canadian People," *Seventh Census of Canada, 1931*, XIII, pp. 769, 775.

[4]Emil Lengyel, *Americans from Hungary* (Philadelphia, 1951), p. 126.

[5]Dominion Bureau of Statistics, *Origin, Birthplace, Nationality and Language of the Canadian People* (Ottawa, 1929), p. 118; Hurd, "Racial Origins," pp. 792, 757.

[6]The Polish peasant family played a similar role among immigrants. W. I. Thomas and Florian Znaniecki, *The Polish Peasant* (New York, 1927), p. 860.

There was no room for picture brides or mail order wives among the Hungarians, and the final decision rested with the young people. Relatives could use persuasion, but not coercion. If the girl did not wish to leave her home or the boy did not like the girl recommended to him, the marriage plan was given up. Hungarian society accepted the principle of marriage based upon romantic love, although the latter had often to be reconciled with the family policy. The special conditions in Canada, however, often forced the immigrant to make his marital selection on the basis of practical considerations rather than on romantic love. In many cases bride and groom had not met before the bride's arrival in Canada. Their previous intercourse consisted of a meagre correspondence and the exchange of a few pictures. Whether romantic love, rational considerations, or persuasion of relatives was the main motive of selection, the marriages usually turned out well. Life in a strange country linked husband and wife with powerful ties. As one respondent put it: "Where there was no love before marriage, it came afterwards."

The immigrant had to overcome many obstacles in order to obtain a "good" wife, and his marriage had to be prepared for a long time and with a great purpose-directedness. Two case histories will be illuminative in this respect.

A. came to Canada at the age of 25, at the height of the depression. For many years he did not intend to marry, but wanted to "enjoy life" and "play around with girls." As the years passed on, he slowly "matured," but when he finally decided to get married, the war halted Hungarian immigration. Nevertheless, he began to "straighten out the affairs" and to establish the financial basis for marriage. Quitting his factory job, he went into landscape gardening and became prosperous. As soon as the war was over, he wrote "home" and asked the relatives to find a suitable girl. They recommended a very good-looking girl, 16 years his junior, who was willing to come to Canada. Before her arrival, A. purchased a large rooming house and he "did not count the money" when furnishing it. Upon her arrival he received her with "everything one can desire." In spite of the considerable age difference, their marriage appeared to be a happy one, and the financial comfort offered by A. may be an important factor in the happiness.

B., a poor bachelor, has been unsuccessful in his marriage plans. When emigrating, he left behind a "selected girl," but the girl grew impatient and married another boy. After that B. took up correspondence with "the girl next door" in the home village, but it did not come to marriage either. Later he courted the daughter of a Hungarian farmer and wanted to propose to her. But the farmer "struck rich" and the financial difference made marriage impossible. Finally he mentioned the name of a Hungarian widow. Very likely there has been a long courtship, but no marriage. B., 47 at the time of our interview, seems doomed to stay a bachelor.

As the case histories indicate, similar factors are instrumental in both financial and marital success. No wonder that the greatest scarcity of females coincided with the worst economic situation. In the 1930's the Hungarian group was very much like a camp of lonely males. Stories were told from this time about a rooming house where more than ten men lived and the only woman resident was the operator's wife. "There were plenty of girls around," commented another respondent, "but they were for guys with money." Some casual remarks recall the atmosphere of those years. One of the members said: "Some of the men went simply crazy. They squandered a fortune on whoring." A few others, and they seem to represent the majority of the group, complained of those "bitter" years "when there were no girls around." One added: "It was a dog-life."

The years spent under such unnatural circumstances must have left some lasting effects upon the immigrants. The situation became a main source of frustration, and the frustration complex is important in the psychology of immigrants. Beneath the surface of recently achieved economic success and good adjustment, the remnants of old frustrations can be detected, and the sexual deprivation, suffered for many years, must be named as one reason.

Changes in Paternal Authority

The European family, as has been often noted, still retains many traits of the patriarchy such as the great authority of parents over children, and of husband over wife.[7] It should be added, however, that family life in Europe is less uniform than in America and it shows a wide range of variations according to nations, classes, religions, and other dividing factors.

In Hungarian society the prevailing patriarchal type of family showed as many forms as there were classes in the society. The lower-middle-class family displayed the strongest paternal authority; the children's life centred around that of the parents, and the whole family made common efforts for advancement. The proletarian class comprised many disorganized families where paternal authority had been broken down and where the family organization approached that

[7]E. W. Burgess and H. J. Locke, *The Family* (New York, 1945), p. 180; Thomas and Znaniecki, *The Polish Peasant*, pp. 87–106; Donald Young, *American Minority Peoples* (New York, 1932), chap. x; G. E. Simpson and J. M. Yinger, *Racial and Cultural Minorities* (New York, 1953), chap. xvi. Concerning the Canadian scene see Frank E. Jones, "The Newcomers," *Food for Thought*, March 1954.

of the Negro matriarchal family in America. The middle-class family was the nearest approach to the American equalitarian family; it granted the greatest freedom to children, applied the least corporal punishment and restricted the usual authority of sib people. As for some other factors, paternal authority was stronger in the rural than in the urban population, stronger in the Protestant than in the Catholic families, and stronger in families which were socially ascending.

The patriarchal family was regulated by ancient customs. Many familial customs of twentieth-century Hungary can be traced back to the Hungarian customary law as codified by Verböczi in 1514. In modern times, of course, the customs were affected by influences similar to those that transformed the patriarchial family of the Puritan settlers into the equalitarian American family of our day. In European societies, however, the transformation progressed slowly and gradually. The family system proved to be elastic and reconciled the innovations with the customary traditions. No open clash emerged, and family life did not become a public problem as it did in America.[8]

Custom defined everyone's role in the family. The father was regarded as the representative of the family to the outside world. To him belonged the right of final decision on every important issue, particularly in financial matters; in the lower-middle class and in the peasantry he acted as the main purchasing agent of the family. The same customs, however, set up certain rules requiring him to act with care and dignity. He had to exert his prerogatives for the common benefit of all members; he had to show his constant love and affection; and for important decisions he had to consult his wife, the grown-up children and sib people. Customs built up a strong safeguard against the abuse of paternal authority.

The wife's role has never been restricted to the household only. Even in old times, with or without legal reasons, wives often assumed the leadership of the family. In modern times, they had a proverbial influence upon politics, business, and community life. They worked as bread winners, managed large estates and business undertakings. Many families had to thank one of these practical-minded women for their social success.[9] However, Hungarian women have never established successful formal organizations comparable to those of American

[8]Béla Radvánszky, *Magyar családélet és háztartás* (3 vols., Budapest, 1879–86); Sándor Márai, *Egy polgár vallomásai* (2 vols., Budapest, 1934); József Darvas, *Egy parasztcsalád élete* (Budapest, 1935); Gyula Illyés, *Lélek és kenyér* (Budapest, 1939).

[9]Ida Bobula, *A nö a XVIII. század magyar társadalmában* (Budapest, 1933); Lajos J. Illyefalvi, *A kenyérkeresö nő Budapesten* (Budapest, 1930).

women. The newspapers did not carry women's columns and when, under Anglo-Saxon influences, a few emancipated women tried to organize female veto groups, their attempts failed.

The children's role was a specific one. The American equalitarian family is willing to regard children as equals of the grown-ups, permitting them great independence in managing their own affairs, and making serious efforts to ensure them equal rights in shaping the family life. In Hungarian society, full status was attributed to the grown-ups only, a stage reached not earlier than about 18 years of age in the lower classes and 22 to 25 years of age in the upper ones. Up to this age the children were looked upon as immature, undeveloped beings who could not participate in important decisions. The growing child had to be prepared for his adult life; he had to be guided, educated, and supervised by parents and sib members. The parents' duty was to give "good preparation for life." The children's duty was to follow with reverence the older people, particularly the parents and relatives.

Parents and relatives made certain that the children's behaviour should be "proper" and that they "should not bring shame upon the family." Achievement at school, the selection of an occupation, and particularly the marriage of the children were the common concern of the family. However, supervision was exerted, and obedience rendered, in an informal, customary way which did not stifle the will of the children. Young people frequently married against the wish of their parents, such a case being the ideal example of romantic love as conceived by Hungarian society.

The control of parents over children was motivated by love and care, and the emotions which linked the members of the family were manifested at every occasion. It could be hardly said that Hungarian parents loved their offspring more than Americans do. However, Anglo-Saxon etiquette demands reticence in the display of the affections, to hide them before strangers and to suppress them in the intimate circle of the family. Hungarians, on the other hand, freely exhibit their affectionate emotions, even before strangers or in public places.[10] The family education aimed not to suppress, but rather to unfold this emotional life, and every major event of family life was accompanied by a free display of emotions, kisses and tears. Hungarian

[10]A Hungarian father of middle-class origin complained about the "Canadianization" of his 13-year-old son: "He does not want to be kissed. He is ashamed of it. He still allows his mother to kiss him at night, but he objects whenever I want to kiss him."

children undoubtedly received more smacking and more kissing than American ones. But even the most severe punishment was accompanied by so many emotions that no child felt it as a despotic cruelty. Parental control was easily accepted because it was surrounded by an affectionate atmosphere.

Many continental societies granted special prestige to age because of the greater experience and knowledge given by years. In the Russian peasantry "the authority of the major of the household was respected on the ground of his greater experience, which comes with age, as well as of his administrative ability."[11] In Hungarian society the father was supposed to act as the wise leader of the family, and a "good" father made strenuous efforts to live up to such expectations. The ideal type of mature man was supposed to possess not only some factual knowledge, but a certain wisdom and common sense which could be applied to the practical questions of life. He was expected to reach a decision in a way beneficial to all members of the family. His judgment was believed to be superior to that of women, who were considered to be lacking objectivity, and to that of youths, inexperienced in worldly affairs. Intellectual superiority was a secure basis of the father's status.

Oppressive as such a system may appear to an American observer, it was far cry from parental despotism. The parents did not intend to establish a tyranny at home, and the children grew up not into submissive, but rather competitive individuals. Such a family life prepared the children adequately for that individualistic competition which characterized Hungarian society. On Canadian soil, however, such a family system was as strange as the sib system or the stratification of the Hungarian minority. The immigrant brought it with him as a part of his social heritage and regarded it as the only good type of family. He noticed, of course, that Canadian familial patterns are different, but formed a rather unfavourable opinion of them. One respondent spoke of the American family as "the cradle of sin," another as "the despotism of children," and a third one described it in words which can be shortly rendered as "the disorganization of the family." In spite of such a dislike, they could not resist the pressure of the Canadian environment. Canadian traits gradually crept into the Hungarian family system, its old patterns had to be modified, and the roles of the members rearranged.

[11]Isaac A. Hourwich, *Economics of the Russian Village* (New York, 1892), p. 90, quoted by W. Lloyd Warner and Leo Srole, *The Social Systems of American Ethnic Groups* (New Haven, 1945), p. 104.

Hungarian women in Canada became wage earners engaged outside the home and took over the function of purchasing for the family. In the new country, shopping and handling of money had to be re-learned, and women were in many cases more proficient than men. Many women acquired better English than men[12] and developed great versatility in shopping. Soon they accepted the role of handling the family's finances and proved to be valuable collaborators, often the main promoters, in the family saving plan. "A woman's hand holds the purse tighter," said one man. Acting as the "finance ministers" of the families, women collected the rent in the rooming houses, did banking and watched all the expenditures.

Immigrant women made a great step toward the American patterns, but the change was prompted by the necessities of life rather than by a conscious imitation of American behaviour. Hungarian women never wanted to imitate Canadian women or to initiate reforms in the family system. They were satisfied with family life as known in the old country.

Children and Parents

The situation is very different with the children. The children were reared amidst the patterns of the immigrant home, but through their playmates and schoolmates they soon gained a good insight into Canadian family life. The school instilled into them the Canadian system of values with its important reference to the equalitarian family. They soon discovered that the Canadian type of family promises greater freedom, more generous allowances, less etiquette. The picture was alluring, and the children came to like the Canadian forms and tried to imitate them. According to one father, the children are "manageable" up to the age of ten. After that "they want to do things as Canadians do."

As a first sign, the children ask for larger allowances, whereas the parents stick to the old principle that "too much money gets youngsters into mischief." Soon, however, a compromise is reached, and the problem of allowance seldom disturbs the peace of the family. Puberty, however, brings forth some graver problems, real stumbling blocks to the father's leadership. The boys' problem is whether to continue schooling or to take a job; the girls' problems are dating and court-ship.

In Hungary, the best, and often only, channel of advancement was

[12]Such a finding is in conflict with the results of some other studies, e.g., Warner and Srole, *Social Systems of American Ethnic Groups*, pp. 108, 220.

given by education, which opened the door to the higher classes. Immigrants still keep a strong faith in the power of education. Having made money, they want to send their children to higher schools. The great goal of many families is to make a professional man out of the son. The sons, however, show less enthusiasm for such a plan. They share the desire that seems to be rather common among Canadian youth of similar class, to leave school and make money as fast as possible.

This question leads to a certain tension. The parents, supported by the sib, try to persuade the reluctant boy, whereas the boy's attitude is supported by his peer group of schoolmates and other friends. Although the tension may last for several months, usually the Canadian patterns carry the day, and the boy's will prevails. Only those who feel like doing so continue their studies, the others leave school to the great disappointment of the parents. One father said of his son: "He could have become anything, doctor, lawyer, minister, anything. But he didn't like to learn. He never takes a book in his hands. Well, what is he now?"

The coming of age of the girls presents another problem because the Canadian patterns of dating, courtship, and marriage differ from those in Hungary. In Hungary, customs and etiquette restricted the free movement of youths. Dating and courtship began at a later age than in America; schoolgirls were usually not allowed to date; middle-class and even some lower-middle-class girls were chaperoned until their engagement; they had to be at home at supper time. The boy-friend and girl-friend system was unknown, but the youth of both sexes had its own social life within the social circle of the parents. A "good" girl could not be seen with a boy unknown to her parents.

Immigrants try to instill these old-country patterns into their daughters, but their efforts are contrary to the Canadian influences. Immigrants are rather indifferent to the Canadian status system, but it is not so with their daughters. The latter wish to participate in the status competition and to gain "popularity" in the social life as it develops around the high school. Such an ambition brings them into conflict with the cherished patterns of the parents, and a mother related the following incident about her daughter:

She was hardly sixteen when boys started to ring her up. I would not have minded one nice boy, since one must have a boy friend in Canada. But there were several of them, and they kept phoning till late in the night. I told her to stop this phone business, but she never listened to my words. One night we were already sitting at the supper table and she was still talking to her boy friend. I got really mad. I ran out of the kitchen, grabbed the receiver and told the boy that he should stop phoning because my daughter will never be allowed to go around with such no good boy who has nothing to do all the day but phone to girls.

The mother's behaviour was not an unreasonable loss of temper, but fully motivated by the Hungarian value system. In the daily life of the family, however, the old value system cannot be retained for long. A compromise is necessary. A Hungarian farmer put it as follows: "In this country one must allow greater freedom to the girls. But we still do keep an eye upon our daughter." In other words, Hungarian daughters must be at home somewhat earlier; they introduce their friends to the family at an early stage of the friendship; they spend more time at home and are somewhat more controlled than Canadian girls. The differences are rather subtle, and an outside observer would hardly detect them.

Such a compromising attitude prevents serious family conflicts. It seems that in certain ethnic groups the family system lacks the elasticity which is needed to reconcile the two opposing sets of values. The family is unable to solve this problem, and as a result trouble, hostility, and juvenile delinquency appear. The picture of disintegrating immigrant families and of second-generation people torn by culture conflict is rather common in American sociological literature.[13]

Our sample was characterized by a conspicuous lack of conflict between the two generations. Parents and children were related by mutual understanding and affection. The grown-up children would not leave the parental home before marriage, and married daughters with their husbands often shared the home of the parents. No case of juvenile delinquency came to our knowledge, and the members were apparently proud of their "beautiful" family life. One of them remarked: "We don't let loose the family." The following case history, told by a mother, shows that emotionalism and parental authority include the necessary means of social control and are able to maintain such a family system.

Pete is really a good boy, but he made his false step too. All that started when he picked up some friends on X. street. . . . For a week he played

13Florence G. Cassidy, *Second Generation Youth* (New York, 1930), pp. 32–6; Eva R. Younge, "Population Movements and the Assimilation of Alien Groups in Canada," *Canadian Journal of Economics and Political Science*, X (Aug. 1944); C. H. Young and H. R. Y. Reid, *The Japanese Canadians* (Toronto, 1939), pp. 95–6. Earl Lomon Koos (*Families in Trouble*, New York, 1946, p. 37) described a Hungarian family in Yorkville, New York City, with a serious conflict centring around the divergency of the value system.

hookey, but we didn't learn about it. . . . Then one night when I come home I see a policeman before the door. "Where is Pete?" he asks me. "He must be in the school." "No," he says, "he hasn't been in school for a week." At that time I was dying with anguish to learn what the police wanted from my son. "Some boys stole a car," he says, "and we want to question him." Oh, I started to weep like a shower and before my eyes I saw my son in jail. . . . It was late at night when he came home finally. His father grabbed him right away and started to question. His father shouted: "I'll beat you apiece if you don't stop lying." So he admitted that he had been running around with those boys, and some of the boys had stolen a car, but he had had no part in it. My man got really mad, his face was red as red pepper. He took off his belt and started to beat Pete with its happier end [i.e. with the buckle] and shouted: "My son will never turn a criminal. I'll beat him to death sooner. I don't want to have a son in the jail." He gave him a honest beating. He even smashed the lamp with his belt and when he finished, poor Pete was full of blood, and his clothes of bloodstreaks, and the rug of bloodstains. . . . Oh, it was a horrible night. I couldn't sleep one moment because of the tears and sobbed all the time: "My God, what will become out of my son?" On my side my man was sighing just the same way. . . . So next morning Pete came down, his face still looked awful, and we all had our breakfast without a word. Then Pete took his books and left. But he was back in a minute, and his eyes were full of tears, and he couldn't speak and he kissed me and kissed his father and he said: "It will never happen again."

Pete was severely punished amidst a free outburst of emotions. His mother, telling the story several years later, was still affected by the old emotions, and we have tried to render her psychological background by translating some Hungarian phrases word by word. Pete, very probably, was affected not so much by the physical act of beating as by the display of emotions, a strange mixture of love, anxiety, anger and family pride. The tears shed by all members of the family worked as a real catharsis. After the outburst of feelings, Pete's promise of good conduct restored the old love and care.

In the general atmosphere of emotionalism, smacking is given and forgotten fast. However, it does not require a great amount of corporal punishment to maintain parental control. Quite a few interviewees mentioned that they "have not touched their children, not even with one finger" since the age of six or eight. It seems as if the children were willing to submit themselves to parental control. If they have a grievance, they try to reach a new, more favourable compromise, but do not attempt to upset the whole family system.

Emotionalism could be transplanted into the Canadian environment, but the intellectual leadership of the parents encountered greater difficulties. The parents, as most immigrants with a similar education, remain to the end of their lives rather inexperienced in Canadian ways and in the English language. They are "ignorant" in many respects when compared to Canadian parents. They do not read comic books or know the rules of baseball, they are rather poorly informed about the banking system or the geography of the new country. In such fields the children are superior. Actually, they have an important role in the immigrant family as mediators of the Canadian culture, and their help is indispensable when a money order must be made out, an insurance policy translated or an occasional trip arranged.

The fathers, however, can still rely upon the treasures of the old-country folk wisdom. Their financial success clearly proves that they are not helpless in the new country, and their common sense ensures their leadership in the family. They are not the "pals" of the children, as the American father is sometimes depicted, but rather circumspect persons who can be consulted any time. Teen-aged boys do ask for the advice of the father when "having trouble with a girl" or when making an important decision concerning their work. Girls resort even more frequently to their mother's advice in the problems of love and marriage. The advice is often accompanied by persuasion and carries great weight with the young.

Under the influence of the new country the old Hungarian family type has changed in many ways. The role of the members has been rearranged and a general compromise has been worked out between the Hungarian and Canadian family system. The compromise is steadily changing, taking in more and more Canadian traits as the time passes, but the coherence of the family is not weakened by the changes. In Little Sicily of Chicago the Italian family was "going to pieces in the conflict with an alien culture."[14] But the Hungarian family has been saved from such a fate; it has remained a massive unit.

Marriage of Second-Generation People

Common background attracts people to each other and it is no wonder that descendants of immigrants up to the third generation tend to marry into their own ethnic group. Among immigrants of different stock living in a Rhode Island community, intermarriage was found to be 12.1 per cent for the foreign born, 20.9 per cent for the second generation, and 40.4 per cent for the third generation.[15] However, the various ethnic groups differ conspicuously in their marriage behaviour.

[14]H. W. Zorbaugh, *The Gold Coast and the Slum* (Chicago, 1929), p. 188.
[15]Bessie Bloom Wessel, *An Ethnic Survey of Woonsocket, Rhode Island* (Chicago, 1931).

Immigrants from eastern and southern Europe (Slavs and Italians) have a lower rate of intermarriage than the old immigrant stock (British, Scandinavian, and German). Hungarians, both in Canada and the United States, seem to occupy an intermediate position. They have usually a somewhat higher intermarriage rate than Slavs or Italians, which may be due to their smaller number, but a lower rate than Germans, which may be explained by their greater difficulties with language and shorter residence in their new country.[16] Concerning the present situation in Canada, a Hungarian minister estimated that among second-generation Hungarians about two-thirds of the marriages are endogamous. The majority of second-generation people, he estimated, marry among themselves and only exceptionally do they marry a first-generation immigrant. In about one-third of the cases second-generation people marry into other stock.

His estimate was surprisingly well corroborated by facts in the sample group. In the 90 families 131 children were married and 41 of these (31.3 per cent) married outside the group. This rate is considerably higher than that found in Rhode Island twenty-odd years earlier. It is very likely that, because of the better economic position of the immigrant and a generally accelerated process of adjustment, the rate of intermarriage has increased over the last few decades. As it was generally observed, girls show a stronger tendency for intermarriage. Out of the 41 cases, 23 Hungarian brides and 18 grooms selected non-Hungarian partners in marriage. In almost every case the partner selected from the out-group was Canadian-born and in the great majority, of British stock.

The group, apparently, favours in-marriage; Hungarian parents prefer a second-generation Hungarian as an in-law; but they do not reject the idea of intermarriage, except with those groups that are regarded as inferior and with whom marriage is taboo. The attitude of the immigrant family is well reflected by a case history:

The D. family had two daughters. Claire, the older, was 9 months old when brought to Canada; Irene, the younger, was born in Canada, two years after immigration. Both girls finished high school and took up office work. Their personalities, however, showed marked differences. Claire was the favourite of her mother and complied more with parental desires and old-country patterns. Irene displayed greater independence than her older sister and was more Canadian in her social patterns. Such a position in the

[16]Niles Carpenter and Daniel Katz, *A Study of Acculturization in the Polish Group of Buffalo* (University of Buffalo Studies, vol. VII, no. 4, 1929); James H. S. Bossard, *Marriage and the Child* (Philadelphia, 1940), pp. 103, 112–13. See further the Canadian Census Monographs mentioned in note 5.

family might be of importance in her later intermarriage. Claire married a second-generation Hungarian boy whose parents were well known to the D. family. Irene, too, had a second-generation Hungarian boy-friend. The two parent-families, close friends, would have welcomed a marriage. However, the boy's parents decided to return to the old country. The boy hesitated for a while, but finally left Canada with his parents.

After his departure, Irene began to go out with Bob, a student at the university, who came from a middle-class English family in the Maritimes, and lived in D.'s rooming house. When their friendship reached the stage of steadiness, he had to move out in order "to avoid gossip." He rented a room nearby and became a daily guest in D.'s home.

There he was cordially accepted. The friendship with Claire and her husband was easy, since both spoke English as their everyday language. The intercourse with the parents required more effort. Mrs. D. was talkative, and Bob soon learned to understand her strongly accented pidgin-English. Mr. D. had a speech defect, and his English was almost incomprehensible; he often resorted to international gestures in communication. Bob was deeply impressed by the hospitality of the home and stated: "I have never seen such a friendly kind of people. A guest is a king with them. When they first invited me, they asked my favourite dish, and treated me to that." When Bob's mother came up for a get-acquainted visit, she was similarly impressed by the etiquette of hospitality.

By the time of the formal engagement, Bob was acquainted with the sib. In accordance with the etiquette, he addressed all older members as "Uncle" or "Aunt," using the equivalent Hungarian word, and they called him "our younger brother." Incidentally, he became fond of the sib life and enjoyed the great parties. Outside the sib, of course, the young couple followed the usual patterns of Canadian youths. After marriage, the young couple left Toronto. When bidding farewell, Mrs. D. shed tears and kissed "her two children," that is, daughter and son-in-law, several times. The marriage is reported as being "good and happy."

In this case family and sib seemed to promote the intermarriage. They accepted "the English boy" readily and tried to engulf him in their own social organism. His co-operation in this respect was sincerely appreciated. When he complied with the customs of the in-group, all relatives became fond of him. The courtship and marriage were "good and happy" because the young couple tried to accept the Hungarian patterns. They responded to the friendly approaches of the sib in a similar way, although their courtship and later family life followed the Canadian patterns. They were able to work out their own compromise.

The Canadian patterns of courtship and marriage have actually conquered the entire second generation. Shower parties, receptions for friends, display of engagement or wedding presents were social rituals unknown in Hungary, but they are meticulously observed by second-generation people. After the wedding, however, as a particular custom of the group, the young people prefer to take up residence with the parents of the bride.[17] This custom is not a rudiment of some enlarged family system, but rather a financial help given to the young couple; it is a Canadianized form of the dowry.

Dowry was a general custom with all but the poor classes of Hungary. It furnished an important consideration before marriage and enabled many rich girls to marry into a higher social stratum. In Canada the Hungarian families gave up the old custom. Except for a few rich farmers, there is no dowry and the young bride brings with her nothing but her personal belongings, some furniture and household items. However, the room and board offered by the bride's parents is a great financial help. During this period the young couple are supposed to save enough to set up their own household or even to buy their own home. Then they move out. The separation of mother and daughter cannot happen without emotional scenes, kissing and weeping. The separation, however, is by no means final. At first, the young wife "comes home" for a visit or phones almost every day, and the young couple show up almost regularly for Sunday dinner.

However, when the second-generation couple set up their own home, they make an important step on the way of Canadianization. From now on the Hungarian patterns which have been observed in the parental home are slowly abandoned; the ties with the sib people weaken; and the young couple in their new environment gradually conform with all the Canadian patterns. After a few years of independent life they still observe the Hungarian customs when visiting the parental home, but in their own home they live as the other Canadian families do.

The Hungarian immigrant family has maintained some modernized traits of the old patriarchy, but has established a working compromise with the familial patterns of the new country. It is a stricter, stronger unit than the Canadian family of similar class and status, and contributes very much to the happiness of the immigrants. The Hungarian group is extremely atomized in its social structure and is divided into small, often hostile sub-groups. However, it has established its special network of micro-organizations—sibs and families which are the main integrating forces of the ethnic group. When they cease to function, as happens at a certain point in the life of second-generation people, the ethnic group ceases to exist. The offspring become unnoticeable parts of Canadian society.

[17]Similarly, it was a custom with the Italians in Boston that young married couples should live with the parents. Walter Firey, *Land Use in Central Boston* (Cambridge, Mass., 1947), p. 193.

CHAPTER V

CHANGES IN THE FORM OF LIFE

IN HIS ECONOMIC ACTIVITIES the immigrant adopted many Canadian traits which were helpful in competition. In family life, on the other hand, he clung to many cherished traditions of his social heritage and tried to compromise Hungarian and Canadian patterns. Altogether, it seems that the way of adjustment is not a straight path, and the immigrant cannot make the same progress in every field of life. Each field has its own difficulties, which are determined by the relation of the social heritage the immigrant brings from the old country and the patterns he finds in the new one.

The social heritage of the Hungarian contains not only a familial pattern, but a more general, superordinate concept, a form of life. In those continental countries where the remnants of feudalism were strong each class had a special style of life which was conspicuously manifested willingly or unwillingly. The class position of the individual was clearly revealed not only by his general behaviour, but also by such specific characteristics as clothing, housing, nutrition, manners, etiquette, speech, and so on. Everybody had his class and status imprinted upon his appearance. With the aid of such external traits class position could be sized up at the first glance, and unknown persons could address each other with the proper titles.

When the immigrant set foot on Canadian soil, he wore all the visible marks of his class, the poor class. Clothing, hair arrangement, talk and walk, pieces of luggage, habits of eating, housing or washing —briefly, every external trait differed from corresponding Canadian forms and mirrored his social heritage. The immigrant was visibly a hayseed. The Canadian observer must have been struck with his strange appearance. One of the historians of Saskatchewan visited the first Hungarian colony, Esterhazy, in the early years of the settlement. He commemorated the inhabitants with a warm touch, but to his amazement he discovered "Oriental" traits in their way of life; those "Oriental" traits were parts of the form of life of the peasant class in central Europe.[1]

[1]John Hawkes, *The Story of Saskatchewan* (Chicago and Regina, 1924), II, pp. 691–4.

On the other hand, the immigrant was struck by the lack of such outward distinctions in Canada. One of his first impressions was that people here have no form of life, that all people "look alike" and it is impossible to judge anybody's class position by his appearance—a realization which enhanced the natural bewilderment of the recently arrived. Undoubtedly, one of the basic features of American society is that the form of life is pretty much the same for a great part of the population. In spite of considerable differences in income or status, the great mass of the population does not manifest differences in such external traits as clothing, food, manner of speech; the differences in status displayed by houses or cars are of a financial nature only and might be eliminated in a short time through financial success.

After some years in Canada the immigrant became in his appearance indiscernible from the majority of the population. He cast away the form of life of the old country, he took over the clothing, eating, housing and other habits of the Canadians. The process was, to a certain extent, a problem of higher income and changed buying habits. The immigrants had come from a society where forms of the old household economy had been partly maintained. Hungarian peasant families had produced many necessities in the household and had obtained many others through barter or payment in kind, but without actual use of money. The standard of living had been low, in the agrarian proletariat extremely low, and the immigrants' saving plans were greatly aided by the low pretensions they brought along. As the immigrant gained access to the "easy" money in Canada, his pretensions grew. When he reached the saturation point, he adopted by and large the Canadian pretensions. From that time on, his form of life did not differ essentially from that of an average Canadian of similar status; the immigrant, at first bewildered, timid and maladjusted, began to act as a well-adjusted member of Canadian society.

This change was promoted by various psychological motives. The feeling of being visibly strange added to the insecurity of fresh immigrants. It was a feeling of being watched and gazed at, of being unprotected and open to any attack. A change in clothing cured the visible strangeness and brought immediate relief. Canadian "appearance" bolstered self-confidence, removed the danger and paid off in a tangible way. It is generally found that visibly strange immigrants are in a disadvantageous position on the labour market, whereas Canadian appearance opens up the better jobs.

Adjustment in the form of life was of immense significance. It was more than a change in clothing, more than a step in Canadianization; it meant a change in mentality, it meant democratization. Together with his peasant suit the immigrant discarded the Hungarian concepts of the class system; he denied the tenet that everybody must show his social standing in a visible way. He embraced the external traits of an equalitarian society and the principles of equality as well. The change in appearance went along with a change in mentality. The immigrant began to regard himself as equal to anybody and claimed all rights of equality.

In the following part we shall trace the complex process of changes in three important fields—clothing, food and housing.

Clothing

In Hungary, as in many other continental countries, clothing was regulated by an intricate set of customs. Dress, although allowing room for individual variations, had to follow certain norms. Everyone was supposed to wear clothes becoming to his age and social standing. Age could be easily signalled by garments. Old people dressed in dark colours with a conservative cut, young ones in light colours with daring cuts. It was more difficult to express social standing by means of clothing. For this purpose an elaborate system had been worked out.

The middle class and the "thriving" part of the lower-middle class followed the international fashion of London and Paris, but minor traits, conspicuous to the experienced Hungarian eye, varied in each stratum. The upper crust had their clothing tailored in London or Paris, the middle class by a good tailor in Budapest. The poorer strata of the middle class, for example high-school teachers, had cheap tailors, and the material as well as the cut clearly revealed the economic condition of the individual. The lower-middle class wore ready-made clothes produced by the garment industry for the masses at low prices, but in accordance with the designs of the international fashion.

The peasantry had different patterns of clothing. They were entirely independent from the international fashion and displayed the same stable clothing patterns without any change for several decades. Their clothing showed many local variations, but, for men, it can be described as consisting of shining black cow-hide boots, black or dark blue "peasant cut" suit, white shirt with coloured buttons—conspicuously different from the shirts of middle-class persons—and no neckties, the latter being one of the particular items of the higher classes. Even this peasant clothing was articulated according to social strata. The quality of the material or of the boots revealed such fine detail as whether their bearer belonged to the rich, medium or poor stratum of the peasantry.

Some parts of the peasantry, particularly in remote and poor provinces, maintained the locally differing folk costumes. Folk costumes featured in many European countries as a special attraction for visiting tourists. They consisted of hand-made, colourful, and often very artistic garments showing the creative taste of the "folk." Their style was independent of the international fashion. It was an old-time style once proudly worn by the upper classes, then gradually handed down to the poor ones where it was accepted and kept without great changes for a hundred years. As it was rightly stated: "Folk cultures are in part an elaboration of the past. The embroidery on the bodice of a Ukrainian peasant girl represents hundreds of years of elaboration and infinite variations like those on a simple musical theme."[2]

Folk costumes were remnants of the pre-capitalistic household economy when clothing was produced at home. In the present century, a growing number of peasants abandoned them and donned the "city garment" produced by industry and purchased in stores. The disappearance of the folk costume would have been much faster, but certain agencies of the state and politics officially supported their wear and, in many cases, simply imposed them upon the "folk." The ruling class and the patriotic leaders were in favour of folk costumes and branded their relinquishment as "unfaithfulness to the fatherland."

The "Hungarian costume" which is often displayed by immigrants at national festivals and photographed by American newspapers has not very much in common with the "folk costume." The "Hungarian costume" is a fancy dress contrived for the purpose of patriotic meetings. Its style shows a medley of various, often non-Hungarian elements and was greatly influenced by the stage costume of the late nineteenth century. This "Hungarian costume" has never been worn by the "folk," but only by school children, by people in the lower grades of the civil service, and by other lower-middle-class patriotic leaders.

Finally, the proletarian class, the most numerous part of Hungarian society, was characterized by the lack of any fashion or style. Having neither means for dressing, nor status in the national society, their clothing was the rag or the second-hand garment. Their economic inertia prohibited them from participating in the changes of any of the fashions.[3]

[2]Henry Seywerd, "Roots Run Deep," *Food for Thought*, Jan., 1952, p. 22.

[3]Jee János Jankó, *Kalotaszeg magyar népe* (Budapest, 1892), and *Torda, Aranyosszék és Torockó magyar népe* (Budapest, 1893); János Szendrey, *A magyar viselet történeti fejlödése* (Budapest, 1905), and *Adatok a magyar viselet történetéhez* (Budapest, 1908); Károly Kós, *Kalotaszeg* (Kolozsvár, 1932); Elemér

Within such a complex framework it was the function of clothing to represent all shades of the status system and symbolize those qualities which determined the individual's position in society. For example, the clothing habits as they existed about 1940 in the poor and remote village of Rimóc (County Nógrád) reflected everybody's age, marital status, and prestige. The village and some of the neighbouring communities had a particular folk costume. The folk costume was, of course, a Sunday garment only. On working days the patched up odd pieces, common in the poor class, were worn. But on Sunday morning when marching to the church, the whole village was dressed up properly.

A Sunday mass was colourful indeed. The first pews from the altar belonged to the local members of the lower-middle class (notary, teachers, operator of the government controlled chain-store, officials of a near-by large estate) who with their lower-middle-class clothing and in their prominent seats proudly displayed their position at the peak of the local social pyramid. The following pews belonged to the peasants, the left side, facing the altar, to the women, the right to the men. The seats and dress were arranged according to age and status. First came the old women, dressed in black blouse, black skirt and their heads bound with a black scarf; in summer all of them, even the rich ones, came barefoot. The young wives, sitting behind the old ones, wore colourful dresses, colourful scarfs, blouses and skirts; they put on shoes and some of them even stockings. Some of them had clothing purchased in the store, representing the commercialized form of the peasant dress. However, others displayed the folk costume of the village, and the same folk costume was generally worn by all the girls of marriageable age.

Unmarried girls, sitting in the last pews or standing behind them, had their own status symbol which was the most beautiful part of the folk costume. They did not put a scarf on their head since, according to a general custom of the Hungarian peasantry, only married women had to "bind" their head with a scarf. Their blouses were white or light-coloured and beautifully hand-embroidered. This beauty was supposed to prove the domestic skills of the girl. They wore several wide and colourful skirts, up to 12 one over the other, which bounced at every step. The number of skirts represented the wealth of the girl since the heavily embroidered pieces, although home-made and often

Czakó *et al.*, eds., *A magyarság néprajza* (Budapest, 1933–7), I, pp. 381–435. From sociological point of view see Zoltán Szabó, *A tardi helyzet* (Budapest, 1936), and *Cifra nyomoruság* (Budapest, 1938); John Kosa, *Pest és Buda elmagyarosodása* (Budapest, 1937), pp. 223–7, and *A magyar nacionalizmus kialakulása* (Budapest, 1937), p. 11.

inherited from mother or older sister, were expensive in the financial
terms of these people. The footwear of the girls was equally important.
The rich ones had red boots, and red boots were the most expensive
items of all clothing. Other girls had black or red shoes, sometimes
even "city shoes," but a girl of good standing would not have appeared
barefoot in the church.

Girls under the dating age, that is, the age group from 12 to 16,
displayed a simplified folk costume with less and inexpensive embroidery, fewer skirts, and some pieces of "city clothing," and most of
them came barefoot. However, they put colourful ribbons in their
hair which symbolized their social status. Girls under 12 years, standing with their school, had no status and no special rules for dress.
They wore all kinds of clothing, mostly odd pieces inherited from
older members of the family, and went around barefoot. Whereas the
appearance of a marriageable girl was common concern of the whole
family and she was helped in her Sunday dressing by mother and
sister, the clothing of little girls was of no significance.

Men's apparel was regulated by equally intricate customs and
differentiated according to age, social and marital status. Prestige
was conspicuously signalled, and a boy of courtship age was easily
distinguishable from a young married man.

The clothing, as well as the place occupied in the church, accurately
revealed everyone's social standing. When a girl, at the age of 16, put
off her ribbons and took on many skirts, it was a sign to the whole
community that she was entering the dating age and accepting the
courtship of the boys. From then on the community could not object
to her walking with a boy in a lonely lane. Similarly, when a woman
abandoned colourful dresses and took on the black garment, she
openly professed that she was becoming "old." Such an act, however,
was not only a self-renunciation, an open withdrawal from sexual
competition, but the passing into another status. With the same act
she acquired the prerogatives of the "women in the black," that is, the
control over mores, customs, and behaviour.

Thus, the system of clothing provided an effective control of the
community over its members and expressed status of all. The girls in
Rimóc wore the many skirts or the boys the embroidered aprons
proudly as signs of their status and personality. Similarly, the arriving
immigrant regarded his strange clothing as the proper symbol of his
status in the old community, as the extension of his personality. As
long as the traditions of the Hungarian village community were strong,
such a belief had a firm hold over him. In old times, indeed, several

years passed before the immigrant became prone to change his old-country clothing for the Canadian one.

The old immigrant who arrived prior to 1925 kept his peasant clothing in the Canadian environment for a long time. He settled in the Prairies, often in a Hungarian settlement where his compatriots had similar customs and beliefs. In the international medley of the Prairies many other folk costumes were maintained; the territory had no uniform norms of clothing. On the dispersed farms and in the ethnic churches, hardly connected with other parts of Canada, the national peculiarities lived undisturbed. Up to the 1920's, then, old-country clothing was "pretty common" among the Hungarians in western Canada. Old pictures testify of its wide use. A picture from about 1910, taken of the visit of the provincial minister and the Austro-Hungarian consul at a Hungarian settler's farm in Saskat-chewan, shows the two "gentlemen" dressed according to the inter-national fashion. Between the visitors, standing before their log cabin, the Hungarian couple, still clad in the old peasant clothes, presents a startling contrast. Another picture, taken in 1903 of a group of Hun-garian settlers in the Prairies, shows a mixture of Hungarian and Canadian dress, the Canadian one being worn by the majority. In some other family pictures the older generation was wearing old-country clothing, but their children wore Canadian styles. Hungarian clothing has been limited to the immigrant generation only.[4]

The long survival of Hungarian dress in western Canada is signifi-cant because it was difficult for the immigrant to obtain Hungarian garments. Although a few stores in New York City and one in Winni-peg carried European peasant clothes, mail order purchase was difficult for these people, many of whom were illiterate. Thus, a part of the clothing was prepared in the household by the ever busy women. Another part was obtained from the old country, and a piece of clothing received from the home village was the object of special pride. According to a story, a Prairie farmer ordered a pair of boots from the famous bootmaker in his home village. In the troubled times following World War I he patiently waited three years till he received the new boots. However, the emotional attachment that surrounded the clothing traditions of the old country compensated for the time and expense.

After 1930 Hungarian clothing disappeared for good. By that time the Hungarian settlements ceased to be closed colonies, and were

[4]Jenö Ruzsa, A kanadai magyarság története (Toronto, 1940), pp. 83, 132, 462–3, 501. The "Hungarian fancy dress" can be seen ibid., pp. 74, 144.

participating in the brisk life of the Prairies. Old-country clothing became strange, and the second-generation people, by that time grown-up and Canadianized, urged their parents to become "civilized." The *coup de grace* was delivered by the depression when old-country clothing turned out to be expensive when compared to Canadian clothing. After the depression, Hungarian dress was not revived. At the Sunday mass of the ethnic church the car became the object of pride; it took over at least a part of the status symbol of the old clothing. About 1950, "a few old people" on the Prairies still kept "a good, old Hungarian garment in the chest." However, it was no more used, but stored up "to serve as burial dress."

Among the immigrants who came after 1925 the disappearance of the old-country clothing was more dramatic. As a matter of fact, few of them arrived in peasant dress. After 1920 the old traditions were rapidly disappearing in Hungary, in spite of government interference. Many emigrants had purchased "city garments" before setting out for the great journey. However, in those urban centres of eastern Canada to which these people tended, even this kind of clothing proved to be visibly strange. Here strict norms of clothing were observed, partly created by the fashion business, and the immigrant had to conform. One Hungarian related his experience in a few words: "On my first walk [in Hamilton, Ont.] the whole city stared at me. My second walk led me into a store where I bought a complete Canadian outfit for $5.00." Under such circumstances the change to Canadian clothing was a question of weeks only, and nobody thought of ordering another Hungarian suit from the old country. On the Prairie farms the Hungarian dress was kept and worn for sentimental reasons for a long time. In eastern Canada the competitive, urban conditions broke down any sentimentality quickly. As one of the respondents put it: "You simply couldn't get a job in [Hungarian] clothes." City life is not as patient with ethnic peculiarities as the farming country.

Hungarian immigrants have nowadays the same appearance as other Canadians of similar class. Their women display a somewhat conservative taste, they "don't care much for fashion" and prefer to be thrifty in "attire and luxury." The family purchases clothing necessities in stores. Women do much mending and patching, but do not prepare pieces of clothing at home any longer. Clothing is no more a symbol of standing, but a simple commodity, regulated by the market. The elaborate clothing customs of the old country have no more grip on the group. In this field, complete Canadianization has been achieved.

Food

Culinary and eating habits make up another part of the immigrant's social heritage. Communities generally develop their peculiar customs concerning food, and every nation in Europe has its own cooking, its national dishes, drinks, and customs of eating. Because of such national characteristics, culinary pleasures often become associated with the concept of the home country. A dish, a drink, or a festival may turn into the symbol of the fatherland or the community. Eating is an important part of patriotic feelings. Poets dedicate poems to national dishes, and writers and philosophers travelling abroad remember the old country when tasting their national dish.[5]

In this sense there was "Hungarian cooking," an object of national pride and concern. Good food played an important part in the national hedonism, and housewives took pains to live up to the standard. Hungarian eating was characterized by many, copious meals, featuring a rich variety of dishes prepared according to handwritten cook books of the family. An ample use of lard and the national spice, paprika, characterized many dishes. Important meals were accompanied by wine.[6]

At the same time, however, eating habits were articulated according to social classes. The upper crust preferred "French" or "English" cooking. The "Hungarian kitchen" was cherished by a great part of the middle class and the prosperous strata of the lower-middle class, and many good reasons limited it to the higher income brackets. Good "Hungarian" cooking required not only family traditions where the famous recipes were bequeathed from mother to daughter, but also great amount of care and work. It took several hours to prepare a proper dinner. Altogether, good "Hungarian" food was rather expensive and suited those housewives who could afford the assistance of servants.

At the lowest end of the social ladder, the proletarian class was characterized by the same poverty in its food habits as in its clothing. The monotonous diet of the agricultural labourer consisted of bread, cured bacon and soup, fresh meat being served on special occasions only. The men of this class, although carrying out the heaviest physical labour, were undernourished, and the women in many cases were

[5]Robert Michels, *Der Patriotismus* (München, 1929), pp. 74–82; Natalie Joffe, *Hungarian Food Patterns* (Washington, 1943); Kosa, *A magyar nacionalizmus*, p. 11, and *Pest és Buda elmagyarosodása*, pp. 220–3.

[6]A good collection of Hungarian recipes was published in the English language by Charles Gundel, *Hungarian Cookery Book* (London, 1937).

ignorant of those famous recipes which were regarded as "national" dishes.[7]

In spite of such a divergence in the form of life, the immigrant brought over a preference for certain dishes and flavours characteristic of Hungarian society. The preference is still living, and the years spent in Canada have been unable to repress it. The sample group was unanimous in praising "Hungarian" cooking. The national food became an important part of their patriotic feelings towards the old country. One of the most attractive features of parties and picnics arranged by Hungarian churches and clubs is the national dishes and drinks. According to a Hungarian bookseller, the best-seller in the group is—the Hungarian cook book.

However, many families in the sample group follow "Canadian" cooking and feature Hungarian dishes on Sundays only. This strange contradiction must be attributed to the changed position of women. The women who are engaged outside the home do not find time enough to prepare the more elaborate Hungarian dishes. When they return from their jobs, they want to serve a supper which is fast and simple. They resort to canned food and ready mixes as well as to the simpler Canadian recipes. Hungarian dishes are served on Sundays when the housewife has more time or when the holiday calls for a festive dinner. However, families where the wife is not engaged outside the home stick to "Hungarian" cooking.

Housing

Housing in Hungary mirrored a social stratification similar to that of clothing and eating. From the luxurious villas and apartments of the middle class down to the overcrowded tenements of the urban proletariat or to the one-room dwelling given by the landlord to the agrarian proletariat, every class had its specific form of housing.[8] The immigrants, hailing from the poor classes, had lived under the poor conditions of their class; having inherited low pretensions, they could endure a slum in Canada as a necessity or as a means of saving. After some years, however, when they purchased "nice" homes, they conformed with Canadian patterns. Their homes were furnished with Canadian-style furniture unknown in Hungary (Chesterfield, table lamp, standing ashtray). They used the home in the Canadian way,

[7]Concerning the nutrition of different classes see Elek Sopronyi, *A kultursarok gondjai* (Budapest, 1940); László Kerbolt, *Beteg a magyar falu* (Budapest, 1934); Andor Németh, *A naposabb oldalon* (Budapest, 1937).

[8]Tibor Mendöl, "Alföldi városaink morfológiája," *Tisia*, 1936; the papers of Virgil Bierbauer (*Nouvelle Revue de Hongrie*, 1941, 1942).

allotting to every member of the family a separate room—a system unknown to the poor classes in Hungary. They became fond of these improvements and would show their homes and furniture with great pride to visitors. Compared to the overcrowding and poverty in the old country, their homes are good evidence of their higher standard of living.

At the same time, however, they still like the Hungarian style of housing, not, of course, the proletarian tenements or the retainers' shacks on the large estate, but the spacious, solidly built homes of the rich peasants in Hungary. At a party, a well-to-do immigrant described the dream house where he would like to retire; it was the typical house of a rich peasant. Although the other guests shared his emotional attachment, they immediately retorted: "It's no good in this country. Suppose you want to sell it. Who gonna buy it? People here don't like this kind of house. You would lose your money."

Actually, no immigrant tried to build a house in the Hungarian style. If he made more money, he moved into a better and larger, but a "Canadian," home. Under Canadian influences not only clothes, but even homes became regarded as commodities. In stable continental societies, the house, owned by the same family for more than one generation, was regarded as a symbol of the family. It usually carried the name of the family, and the owner clung to it almost as tenaciously as to an inherited farm. Americans, on the other hand, regard a house as an investment that can be sold at any time for profit. Newcomers from continental Europe are always amazed to see how fast people buy and sell their homes. The immigrant was quick to realize this American aspect of home ownership. He saw that he would risk his competitiveness if he adhered to the European traditions. He adopted the investment aspect of home ownership and bought and sold homes as the "little fellow's speculation." Consequently, he wanted the Canadian standards in housing which could be easily sold on the current market. His sentimental longing for a Hungarian style home is a leisure-time phantasy which does not govern his economic activity. This sentimental attachment is shaped by unforgettable childhood memories, but economic activity is determined by adaptation to the market. It is a condition of his success that the two attitudes should be strictly separated.

The immigrant's form of life changed fast and almost completely. His sentimental attachment to old-country traditions has been loosened to a great, but varying extent. In clothing his attachment became almost extinct, in housing it appears as a rather hazy longing for certain Hungarian forms, and in food the strong sentimental preference for Hungarian flavours is still living. However, even sentiments may have their motivation. In clothing it was the feeling of being visibly strange, in food the comfort and the changed role of women, in housing the speculative consideration that molded the immigrant's sentiments. In the final analysis, it was the desire for successful competition which prompted him to conform with the Canadian patterns of life.

American society has created certain agencies which educate people for competition and success. One of the agencies is advertising, and its effectiveness among immigrants cannot be underestimated. Clothing, food, and housing are, in our economy, necessarily tied up with those marketable commodities which are mass-produced by a giant-size industry and promoted through ubiquitous advertising. Advertising functions among immigrants as an important promoter and teacher.[9] Bills, posters, and signs accompany the immigrant everywhere in Canada and serve as the first teachers of English. There is hardly a Hungarian farm in Ontario without the catalogue of the large department stores in Toronto. Usually it can be found in the kitchen, proving that both the housewife and the master of the house like to thumb it in their spare minutes. The effects of newspaper advertising seem to be even more important. An English daily paper comes into every home of the sample group, and some rich farmers "keep" two papers.[10] And it is not only the second-generation people who read them. Among the immigrants, the men prefer Hungarian papers, which furnish "better" information on politics, a topic of general interest; but the women are regular readers of English papers, partly because of their function as purchasing agents of the family.

The women agreed that advertisements are the parts of the newspapers they like best. Although they have a certain interest in sensational stories, weather reports or household advice, they never read those features generally read by Americans, such as comic strips, sport pages, death and birth notices or women's columns. But the advertisements are read systematically. Advertisements of the big department and chain stores, of food and household commodities, of clothing and

9Robert E. Park, *The Immigrant Press and Its Control* (New York, 1922), chap. v; C. A. Dawson, *Group Settlement: Ethnic Communities in Western Canada* (Toronto, 1936), pp. 130–1.

10Out of the three dailies in Toronto, the *Star* was exclusively read by the group. At the time of our research, it was cheaper than the two other papers; it was generally regarded as the paper of the lower income classes; and it showed in its news columns a great interest in the affairs of immigrants.

special sales are equally popular. If a purchase of great importance (farm, home, business, etc.) is planned, they will study the advertising pages for weeks and months.

As one attractive point, advertisements give information about prices and greatly help in saving. One housewife explained: "Every Saturday I would go to the market. Then I would figure out from the paper how much I saved." Another woman pointed out: "There is always some good sale on in the city. You lose if you don't rush there at the right time." As a matter of fact, the women are "sale-conscious" and like to make use of cut-rate prices. More important, advertisements teach many patterns of the new country. The Chesterfield, table lamp or toaster, now common in every household, were not familiar in the old country, and no refrigerator, electric range or even car was used in the poor rural areas. Advertisements taught the immigrant about such commodities. Moreover, they claimed that American commodities are nicer, more useful or less expensive than those to which they were accustomed in the old country. With such persuasion, advertising fulfills an important role in the process of adjustment. It is perhaps the only institutional attempt to counterbalance the emotional attachment to the social heritage. It makes the buying habits of immigrants conform to those in Canada. Members of the sample recalled the early times when their English was imperfect and they entered the store with the advertisement clipped out from the paper, showing it to the sales girl: "Give me this here."

Beyond the practical teaching of what and where to buy, advertising conveys other, more important messages which, actually, are basic principles of the American creed. These messages teach people to long constantly for better things and higher standards of living; they put almost everything before the eye and, through suggested payment plans, within the reach of everybody. Such teaching was particularly attractive to the immigrant. Though he landed in Canada penniless and without pretensions, he gradually began to reach out for the different coveted commodities, for the higher standard of living. Advertising had an eminent part in raising the originally low pretensions. Once, while we were interviewing a group member, his wife was "looking at" the paper and stopped at the advertisement of silver tableware. She pointed to it saying: "I think, Michael, we need such a set." Another woman, who had spent her first years on a farm, related of that time: "Sunday afternoons I thumbed through the old papers of the farmer and longed for the nice things I saw." A mother put it this way: "Whenever I see those charming children in the paper, I immediately wish mine would look as they do." As a striking example of the same general desire we saw a young boy in complete Hopalong Cassidy outfit playing cowboys with his mother—in Hungarian.

Assimilation of the immigrants became more complete in those fields of life which are tied up with marketable commodities, advertising, and other factors of economic competition, a finding which points to the mainspring of the assimilation process in America. In continental Europe, assimilation of minorities is first of all a political problem, and the political agencies, particularly the state, are prone to pursue a vigorous policy. In Canada and in the United States the assimilation of immigrant groups has been primarily a non-political problem. The state has not followed any programme, and Canada's policy is to promote and to maintain the specific culture of immigrant groups. However, the conditions created by a competitive society urge the immigrants to comply with the form of life of the majority. There is no divergent way of competition, and no immigrant group can succeed with the methods inherited from the old country. There is no turning back on the road to success, and the immigrant, once started on this road, marches ahead. From the first moment of his arrival up to the last one spent in the new country, he is in a steady process of assimilation, taking over more and more patterns of the new country. Immigration cannot have only a temporary effect. It changes the personality constantly and irrevocably.

CHAPTER VI

THE SYSTEM OF NORMATIVE
VALUES

THOSE CUSTOMS that regulated the form of life in Hungary were not
haphazard creations of a whimsical society. Behind the customs stood
a system of beliefs and rationalizations, a certain ideology, characteristic of Hungarian society. This ideology asserted that the customs, as
they existed, were just, useful and necessary; that everyone was right
who acted in accordance with the customs, and everyone was wrong
who destroyed them. In this respect the customs were identified with
the normative values. They were regarded as social embodiments of
morality.

The system of normative values in Hungarian society was essentially
the same as that common in Western civilization. Within the cultural
unit of Western civilization, however, national societies, social classes
or religious groups developed their own mores, showing conformity
in the main points, but differing in the details. Both Canadian and
Hungarian societies accept a system of normative values which
originated in Christian ethics and have undergone similar changes
during the historical development of Western civilization. In some
respects, however, different norms came to be accepted by the two
societies. The normative values of Canadian society have been greatly
influenced by Puritanism. In Hungary, on the other side, movements
of religious rigorism (Puritanism and Pietism among Protestants,
Jansenism among Catholics) recruited a few followers, but have never
penetrated the masses. In modern times, the normative attitude of
Hungarian society has been decisively shaped by Josephinism with its
rationalistic morality, and the laity has been greatly influenced by the
hedonistic philosophy of the *Biedermeier*.[1]

The sub-cultures of Hungarian society developed their own varia-

---

[1]See Robert Michels, *Sittlichkeit in Ziffern* (München, 1928). Concerning
Hungary see Lipót Nemes, *A bűnöző társadalom kialakulása* (Budapest, 1935);
Antal Meszlényi, *A jozefinizmus Magyarországon* (Budapest, 1936); Béla Zolnai,
A magyar biedermeier (Budapest, 1939).

tions of the common normative code. The middle class, being the claimed or actual successor of the Hungarian "gentry," had a specific system of values, similar to the code of the English squire and to the German *Herrenmoral*. It centred around a special concept, the "honour of the gentleman," and the two English words "gentry" and "gentleman" were adopted by the Hungarian language as eminent proofs of English influences. The prerogatives of the "gentleman" were based on his personal honour. If honour was lost the prerogatives of the status were lost also. The gentleman had to maintain his unblemished honour throughout his life, had to conform with a strict code of behaviour and had to revenge any insult against his honour. A debt contracted in gambling with other gentlemen was a "matter of honour" and had to be paid within forty-eight hours. A failure in payment led to the loss of the gentleman's status; its practical consequences were resignation as officer of the army, emigration to America, or even suicide, although the latter has not been so frequent as fiction around 1900 would suggest. On the other hand, commercial debt was not a matter of honour and the same gentlemen paid their tailors rather slowly without the slightest loss of their status. The requirement that personal honour had to be defended against any insult became the basis of the duelling system which will be described later.[2]

The normative code of the lower-middle class was determined by its great efforts to achieve the level of the middle class. The code emphasized the virtues of solid citizens and put a premium on reliability, dependability, and correctness. The class outdid itself in solidity and morality, in order to conform not only with what could be called the norms of good morals of Hungarian society at large, but with those of the church, the ruling class, or the government party.[3]

The mores of the poor peasantry can be described as the outcome of very keen competition for small gains in an extremely poor, suppressed, and poorly educated class. It approved almost any means that furthered their small-scale competition. It was tinted with strong class-resentment and praised as "virtues" any act of outsmarting or cheating the ruling classes. Since "law has been contrived by the lords," many instances of breaking the law were approved, and people who got into trouble with the law were often helped by the whole village. The very keen competition and general poverty gave birth to highly "immoral" practices such as those revealed by the notorious

[2]See Geyza Farkas' excellent analysis, *Az uri rend* (Budapest, 1911).

[3]Geyza Farkas, *A kis gazda* (Budapest, 1913); Ferenc Erdei, *Futóhomok* (Budapest, 1937).

arsenic mass murder at Tiszazug. In this backward part of the country, a great number of old people, who were no longer useful, or who had bequeathed an inheritance, were poisoned by their next of kin.[4]

Since the great majority of the immigrants who arrived in Canada prior to 1939 came from the poor classes, their inherited attitude must have been that of the poor peasantry. However, as they made money in Canada, they gradually adopted the normative standards of the Hungarian lower-middle class. At the time of our research, the sample group displayed the solid qualities of socially ascending lower-middle-class families. Its members were anxious to avoid any collision with the Canadian law-enforcing authorities, endeavoured to conform with Canadian standards of life and showed a cautious conservatism in their general attitude. With such qualities the group approached more closely the attitude of the Hungarian lower-middle class than that of their own parents.

Criminality

Criminal statistics permit certain conclusions concerning the behaviour of immigrant groups. They indicate that foreign-born people in America commit, in proportion to their numbers, considerably fewer crimes than the native-born. The former more often commit crimes involving personal violence, but in crimes for gain, including robbery, the rate of the native-born greatly exceeds that of the foreign-born. At the same time the separate immigrant groups differ in criminal tendencies, probably partly because of their imported normative code. Thus, gambling is a respectable business among Italians, and such a code might affect their crime record in this area.[5]

The in-group organization, and particularly the control exerted by the group over the members, is another determinant of criminality. It has been stated that a tacitly accepted principle of Polish-American society is "not to interfere too much with the private life of socially useful members," and this finding was used to explain the social disorganization observed among Polish immigrants in America.[6] On the

---

[4]János Szeberthy-Szeiberth, *Elsodort falu a Tiszazugban* (Budapest, 1935), gives a thorough study of the arsenic mass murder and the normative attitude behind it. See further Gyula Illyés, *Puszták népe* (Budapest, 1935).

[5]T. J. Woofter, *Races and Ethnic Groups in American Life* (New York, 1933), pp. 183–4; Donald Young, *American Minority Peoples* (New York, 1932), pp. 239 *seq.*; William F. Whyte, *Street Corner Society* (Chicago, 1943), p. 140; Arthur L. Wood, "Minority-Group Criminality and Cultural Integration," *Journal of Criminal Law and Criminology*, XXXVII (March 1947).

[6]W. I. Thomas and Florian Znaniecki, *The Polish Peasant* (New York, 1927), pp. 1705, 1538.

other hand, a study of the Hungarians of Detroit disclosed that family relationships and ethnic associations exert a strong control over the moral behaviour of the group. The corrected crime rates of the group were less than the average for immigrants from south and east European countries, and less than half of that for the native white population. The influence of the community is well illustrated by the fact that the rate of juvenile delinquency was much higher for Hungarians who have moved away from their integrated community.[7]

The sample group was not expected to furnish us with reliable numerical data concerning their crime record. As a common human characteristic, people like to be forgetful of their earlier mis-steps, and a respectable immigrant will not reveal any earlier collisions with the law. The life histories, as told to us, were rather silent on any possible criminal act. However, rumours were circulating within the group, rumours which could not be verified. According to the hazy picture they give, quite a few members faced vagrancy charges during the depression; one "had troubles with the police" because of his involvement in a strike; one or two persons were charged with theft; one person was allegedly investigated in connection with arson—a common topic of rumours in the tobacco country; assault, usually involving Hungarians on both sides, was the most common offence mentioned. Except for arson, no serious crime and particularly no conviction for a serious offence was mentioned.

The overwhelming majority of the real or alleged offences took place "in old times," either in the first years after immigration when the newcomer is more susceptible to crime, or during the depression when hard times served as extenuating circumstances. With the end of the depression crime seemingly disappeared from the group. The successful immigrants appear to have been anxious to conform to the law. None of the gossips spoke about crimes committed recently; on the contrary, they emphasized that the same persons are now law-abiding people.

Such fragmentary data would give a rather clean bill to the group. Immigrants, at least those who are not yet naturalized citizens, may face an additional punishment when convicted—deportation. Furthermore, both family and sib exercise a strong control over their members because the crime of one member may bring shame upon the whole sib. The supervision of the youths by relatives tends to cut down juvenile delinquency and, together with some other features of the

---

[7]Erdmann D. Beynon, "Crime and Custom of the Hungarians of Detroit," *Journal of Criminal Law and Criminology*, XXIV (Jan.-Feb. 1935).

family life, is able to counterbalance many criminal tendencies coming from outside organizations such as gangs. The control of the sib regulates the behaviour of the bachelors also, a type which is likely to break the law. As a severe punishment, the offender might be dis-owned and deprived of the valuable help given by the sib. Moreover, sib relationships remove the feeling of being alone, uncontrolled and not responsible to anybody. Thus they overcome a psychological state which might contribute to the criminality of lonely persons.

The Deputy Chief of the Police Department at Toronto stated to us: "We haven't had much trouble with the Hungarians except for some occasional bootlegging or a fight. But no serious offences." How-ever, the law-enforcing authorities were not always of the same good opinion. The Superintendent of the North-West Mounted Police in his annual report written at Lethbridge, 1892, complained lengthily of the "nasty habits" of the Hungarians:

> The Hungarian and Sclavish miners are quarrelsome people and do not get on with each other at all well. They have a nasty habit of bringing long-bladed knives into play; and one such offender would have been eligible for the penitentiary had we been able to complete the evidence against him. . . . Hungarians and Sclavs may be very good miners, but they are not altogether desirable citizens. It is true they keep pretty much to them-selves and wrangle principally with one another, but there have been one or two ugly knife wounds inflicted, invariably by a Hungarian upon a Sclav, for whom he seems to have a contemptuous dislike. The Hungarians are said to have amongst themselves a secret society on the lines of the Italian Mafia, and they dare not give evidence against one another. In prohibition days they used to drink hop beer and become royally drunk on it in course of time; now they mix alcohol with their beer and can attain the desired result much sooner.[8]

The report suggests that the normative attitude of the Hungarian group has changed markedly over the past sixty years. Such a hypo-thesis seems very likely if we assume that the old immigrants of the 1890's brought over the unaltered norms of the poor peasant class in Hungary, whereas in the subsequent decades immigrants have become influenced by the "solid" norms of the lower-middle class. Such a change might have been an accompaniment of the financial success achieved in Canada.

The statements of the law-enforcing authorities, made independently and at different times, contain two specific complaints. They speak of drunkenness or occasional bootlegging and of knifing or fighting. It

[8]Quoted by S. D. Clark, *Social Development of Canada* (Toronto, 1942), pp. 410–11.

seems that in these two aspects of normative values the Hungarian and the Canadian attitudes differ considerably. The differences are worthy of investigation.

The Duel and the Fight

It has been noted that among Chinese and Sicilian immigrants old-country patterns of violence, as a means of honourable revenge for some insult, lead directly to crimes of violence.[9] The situation is similar among Hungarians. Their knifing and fighting are tied up with the system of duelling which was common in Hungary up to 1944.

The "modern" duel, a customary means of maintaining the gentleman's honour in Germany or Hungary, is not a direct continuation of mediaeval duelling arranged by the courts and knightly societies. After the knightly duels of the Middle Ages the custom seems to have gone into oblivion.[10] About 1800, however, it was revived, and the duel became a part of the Hungarian upper-class form of life, a customary means to avenge any insult to the gentleman's honour. Since every member of the ruling and middle class was supposed to be a gentleman, a compulsory system of duelling existed for them. Anyone who did not avenge an insult through the usual channels lost his status as a gentleman and had to suffer severe practical consequences. Any derogatory word, such as "silly" or "jackass," or provocative action, such as a slap in the face or unbecoming behaviour towards a lady, called for a fight. In time elaborate codes, determining the gravity of the insult and the rules of procedure applicable to each degree, were formulated. Several codes were printed and the most authoritative one, compiled by Vilmos Clair, was approved by the Army Officers' Casino at Budapest. The experts of the duelling code, who functioned as seconds or members of the Court of Honour, enjoyed high prestige.

Although the formal procedure of the duel became stiffer and more severe, the actual bloodshed became less and less. A few notorious duel cases in the 1880's, resulting in the death of the "innocent" party, shocked the country, and from that time on, state, church, and some social agencies systematically co-operated to restrict the ferocity of duels. In the time of the Regency the rule became accepted that before

[9]Robert E. Park and Herbert Miller, *Old World Traits Transplanted* (New York, 1920), pp. 10–11; Arnold M. and Caroline Rose, *America Divided* (New York, 1948), p. 244. The knifing among the Polish peasantry might be of a similar nature (Thomas and Znaniecki, *The Polish Peasant*, pp. 1185, 1195).

[10]Concerning Germany see Georg v. Below, *Das Duell und der germanische Ehrbegriff* (Kassel, 1896).

carrying out the actual fight, duel cases had to be submitted to an Officers' Casino or Court of Honour and no weapons could be used unless authorized by such an agency. In most cases the actual duel was transformed into a "knightly affair," that is, an honourable settlement without fight, by way of formal protocol issued in accordance with the duelling code. In those few instances where arms were taken up, the parties did not intend to harm each other. The average young gentleman of about 1940 had several "knightly affairs" in his past to talk about, but very few actual duels were fought and bloodshed was a rarity.

Duelling was part of a ruling and middle-class pattern; members of the lower classes could not afford the expense of the ritual. However, many salient features in the form of life of the middle class were imitated by lower classes, and duelling found its inexpensive counterpart in the fights of the peasantry. Tavern brawls and Sunday afternoon fights of youths are general in every country of the world. However, in some parts of Hungary such fights were subject to rules that were popularized forms of the upper-class code of the duel.[11] The claimed or real reason for a fight was an insult to personal honour, occurring easily while drinking. The insult had to be rectified by fighting, and the fight had to be "fair," that is, man against man and with similar weapons (bare hands or knives). But owing to the lack of formal ritual such rules were frequently violated. It often happened that relatives of the succumbing party ran to his aid and a general fight ensued. In certain localities it was a "virtue" if a young man was of fighting spirit, had several fights and carried the scars of them, just as it was in another popularized form of upper-class duelling, the *mensura* of the German students.

Such fights of the peasantry, although common in certain parts of the country, were by no means general. Actually, the fighting habits were mitigated just as were those of the upper-class duel. The number of fights were cut down; in some places they were discontinued; in other places the dangerous weapons (knives, bottles) were put aside and the ferocity generally moderated. By 1940 the fights represented a problem less acute than fifty years earlier.

Immigrants coming from the fighting parts of Hungary brought over a certain set of norms concerning honour, insult, revenge, and fighting. This code was basically different from, or even contrary to, the Canadian norms. It could be maintained where the Canadian influences

[11]Sándor Petőfi's A helység kalapácsa (from the 1840's) describes a tavern brawl and caricatures the knightly behaviour of the peasants.

were not strong, such as in the Prairies about 1890; but in other provinces it had to be modified. Moreover, the mitigation of the fights in Hungary moulded the attitude of the immigrants also. The clergy and some other educated leaders of the ethnic group acted as spokesmen of the influences coming from Hungary. The clergy delivered sermons against fighting and self-administered justice, and one priest is credited with "having eradicated" the fights in his parish. The Hungarian press in America published articles of a similar nature, and some ethnic clubs expelled those members who had picked a fight around the premises. It is very likely that new immigrants were more willing to settle affairs in a peaceful way than those who arrived in the 1890's. Finally, the immigrants grew older and acquired wealth, both factors prompting them to stop fighting.

It may be assumed that since the 1890's fighting has been constantly decreasing. One minister stated that fighting is no longer a problem in his parish. The sample group was of the opinion that in old times "there had been more fights" than now. The stories of the "famous" old fights were still remembered and narrated with pleasure just as the upper class in Hungary liked to remember the famous old duels. A fight that took place in a Prairie town in the early 1930's was related at two parties with epic copiousness. The following case history which omits the complicated political and personal relations involved gives only a fragmentary picture of it.

N. was a wicked man who did not like to work and always tried to live at the expense of others. During the depression he conceived a racket and lived well by blackmailing the other Hungarians of the town. The Hungarians were helpless against his scheme and had to pay him weekly tolerance payments. Finally P., who was at that time organizing a semi-political club for the Hungarians, took the matter in hand. First he spoke to N. and warned him to stop the racket, but N. continued his extortion. Then one night they met in the alley behind the Hungarian club; P. reproached him angrily and N. answered in an insolent way. Immediately a fight broke out. Both were six-feet, two-hundred-pound fellows and "they fought like giants." "The earth quaked under their feet and the people living in the neighbourhood were frightened in their homes." P. had at that time an injured arm and although he kept up valiantly, could not overcome his opponent. The fight lasted more than an hour and was interrupted only by the message that police were approaching the scene. The two fighters departed in the dark, and after that N. never dared to come near the club. The final encounter could not be delayed long. A few weeks later P., with his hand healed, met N. on the open street. "They just started to fight without any words." It was a short, but "terrible" fight and P. carried the day. "He broke all the bones of N."—a figurative expression of the Hungarian language which must not be taken at its face value. The fight, actually, ended with N. running and P. chasing him with threats to beat him again whenever their paths crossed. After that N. disappeared from the town. The Hungarians were relieved from his extortions, and P.'s club became very popular.

The story, told with great relish and with many poetical embellishments, depicts P. as the heroic defender of the oppressed. Another story, relating how two sibs fought each other for a whole night, emphasizes the "sib honour." With such and similar values involved, the fights mirrored in a popularized form the duel system of the upper class. It is of no importance whether N. and P. were moved by personal rivalry rather than by a code of honour. The Hungarians saw in their fight honour, virtue, and heroism, that set of knightly values which has been imported from Hungary and survived in Canada. However, the decade of depression witnessed the last popularity of the fights. As troubles decreased and the road to success opened, the group seemingly settled down to a peaceful life. At the time of the interviews, the great majority of the group was prone to describe the fights among Hungarians as "harmful," "shameful," or even "barbaric," a judgment which certainly was not prevalent twenty or thirty years earlier. In spite of this majority attitude, fighting has not ceased altogether. A minority of the old immigrants and a few newcomers from the lower classes still resort to fighting in the old style; one of them even got into the newspapers.[12] Their behaviour, however, might be regarded as marginal, preserving a pattern that has become obsolete with the majority.

The attitude of the Hungarian group concerning fighting underwent an important change in Canada. The honour code of the old country, essentially incompatible with the principles of Canadian society, was dropped. The majority of the immigrants approached the Canadian attitude; they became cautious in the use of insulting words and did not resort to immediate revenge for verbal assault. In this change of attitude, however, the effects of the Canadian surroundings were only of secondary significance. The main influences came from Hungary; the behaviour of the immigrants was transformed in the same way as that of a large part of Hungary's population. The change in the attitude of the immigrants merely reflected a similar change in the old country.

Drinking Habits

Hungarian and Canadian societies differ basically concerning those norms which regulate liquor consumption. The difference has a long historical background tied up with religious ethics and economic con-

[12]*Telegram* (Toronto), July 21, 1952.

ditions. In Canada, as in other Anglo-Saxon countries, the attitude toward liquor was shaped by Puritan tenets. Drinking was regarded as a moral problem, and complete abstinence as a virtue. Communities and provinces availed themselves of their law-making privileges to restrain weak human beings from the consumption of liquor. With the decline of Puritan influence, deviant behaviour of the individual became common. However, the individual's use of liquor has remained an affair of private taste and has not affected the communal policy.[13]

In Hungary, and in many continental countries, the attitude toward liquor is not regulated by religious ethics. Although drunkenness is condemned as shameful or immoral, drinking has not been regarded as a moral problem, and communities have never tried to regulate the consumption of liquor. Alcoholic beverages are an ordinary part of meals and a necessary accompaniment of social life; in the villages the pub is an important centre of community life. Religious groups, Catholic or Protestant, do not show any differences in this respect. Not even those old Hungarian Puritans, who studied in England and professed a moral rigorism, tried to restrict the ordinary use of alcohol.[14]

In Hungary, wine was one of the most important staple commodities, the main source of agricultural revenue. For long centuries it was the only product which provided the noble or peasant landholder with cash income. Consequently, the vine growers became the *élite* of every social stratum. The cash income derived from vineyards enabled many noblemen to go into politics and public life and play there a more conspicuous role than the grain growers. The vinedressers, being in old times the only experts in agricultural production, formed the highest stratum of agricultural labour.[15] Vinegrowing as an occupation gave prestige and status.

In addition to economic importance, alcoholic beverages assumed an eminent social function. Parties and other social activities were accompanied by the free consumption of beer, liquor, and wine, and the reputation of being a "good host" was another source of prestige.

[13]John Dollard, "Drinking Mores of Social Classes," in *Alcohol, Science, and Society* (Yale University Press, 1945); J. W. Riley and C. F. Marden, "The Social Pattern of Alcoholic Drinking," *Quarterly Journal of Studies on Alcohol*, VIII (1947); R. F. Bales, "Cultural Differences in Rates of Alcoholism," *Quarterly Journal of Studies on Alcohol*, VI (1946).

[14]Jenő Zoványi, *Puritánus mozgalmak a magyar református egyházban* (Budapest, 1911); József Bodonhelyi, *Az angol puritanizmus lelki élete és magyar hatásai* (Debrecen, 1942).

[15]Gyula Szekfü, "A magyar bortermelő lelki alkata," *Történetpolitikai tanulmányok* (Budapest, 1922).

The quality of the drinks as well as the circumstances of serving them expressed the significance of the social occasion and the status of the guests and hosts. The toasts and "blessings" with wine made up an important part of the social rituals. Thus, intricate rules of etiquette were built around social drinking which rather emphasized its social importance than restricted its consumption.[16]

This attitude to liquor has not undergone any noticeable change among Hungarian immigrants in Canada, either Catholic or Protestant. The moral basis of the Canadian liquor laws has remained strange and incomprehensible to all of them, and liquor regulation is the Canadian peculiarity criticized or even ridiculed most often. It was described as "hypocrisy," or "just a business," or in words that could be rendered as "the advertising stunt of the liquor barons." It was remarked that in Canada "liquor laws are strict and drunkards numerous," or "these Canadians make liquor laws, then go home and get heavenly drunk." The last remark would imply that if there is a morality for the Hungarians concerning liquor, it condemns the non-social drink, the habit of drinking alone.

Liquor consumption has maintained its old social functions among the immigrants. A "friendly" Hungarian home always offers a drink to the visitor whenever he drops in. As in eating or cooking, Canadian influences show up in the drinking habits also. Whisky, which was consumed in Hungary by the "Anglo-maniac" upper classes only, is consumed by the immigrants without any class differentiation. Beer, which was enjoyed in Hungary in the pubs only, is now used in the home. The acceptance of such Canadian traits was largely promoted by second-generation people who exert an influence in this field as well as in cooking or clothing.

The rather superficial Canadian influences are, however, only concessions made under the requirements of the new country. The favourite drink of the group is still wine, often dubbed "the national drink." The emotional attachment to "good" Hungarian-type wine is even stronger than to Hungarian food. Wine became the general symbol of the old country. A Hungarian poet in Canada put it in his verse: "I cannot forget thee, O, Hungary, thy wine and wheat, thy plains and hills." There is no festivity without wine; it is an indispensable accessory of the Easter or Christmas dinner, of a wedding or nameday party.

[16]Pál Schiller, *Borfogyasztási szokások* (Budapest, 1940); Károly Viski, *Hungarian Peasant Customs* (Budapest, 1932), pp. 125–34, 140–46; *A magyarság néprajza*, ed. Elemér Czakó et al. (Budapest, 1933–7), I, pp. 37–123.

In spite of such a demand, the immigrant faces serious difficulties in obtaining his favourite drink. Owing to the liquor laws, he cannot get it from the old country. Having no other sources to satisfy their demand, immigrants tried from an early period to grow "noble" Hungarian grapes in Canada, but because of climatic conditions their attempts were doomed to failure. About 1920, when marketing and transportation conditions permitted, it became a custom with the Hungarians to order grapes from California and prepare their wine at home —a favourite leisure-time activity with the group. Since handling of wine needs experience, those few immigrants who brought from the old country the knowledge of vinedressing soon achieved fame with their good wine. They gained prestige in the ethnic group, and prestige seldom goes without special duties. Theirs is to furnish their countrymen with "good wine." The home-made wine is often given away as a present or, as was general in Hungary, is used as a payment in kind. Quite a few vinedressers get odd jobs around their home done for a certain allowance in wine. Finally, there have been cases where the wine was actually sold.

The friendly distribution of home-made wine is a prestige-giving service rendered to the ethnic group, but it may involve a collision with the liquor laws of the province. Since the Hungarian patterns do not make sharp distinction between home consumption and sale of the wine, it is often difficult to define what constitutes an offence in terms of the Canadian liquor laws. A case history will illustrate this point.

R. was a famous vinedresser and S., a Slovak immigrant, used to work around his home for payment in wine. Once, before Christmas, S. dropped in and asked for some wine. R. gave him a demi-john full of wine, and S. left a five-dollar bill on the table. However, when driving home, he made a wrong turn, a police car caught up with him, and the demi-john was found. When questioned by the police, R. asserted that the wine had been made in common by him and S. It was common property and S. was taking home only his own share. Since S. had been working at R.'s place at the time when the wine had been prepared and had not received any payment in money, the police accepted this explanation and dropped the case.

Although R. accepted the money, his action was dictated not by commercial motives, but by personal consideration for an old acquaintance. As he commented upon the case: "You can't leave an old chum without wine for Christmas." His behaviour was correct according to the Hungarian norms. In Hungary, landlords sold wine to their labourers before Christmas, and a similar act would contribute to R.'s prestige within the group.

It is very likely that there are some professional bootleggers in the Hungarian group. Nevertheless, it might be assumed that in many cases the "bootlegging" is not an occupational activity, done for profit, but an in-group service, done in accordance with the social habits of the group. The non-professional bootlegger gets the protection and cover of his countrymen. Although the group is anxious to avoid trouble with Canadian law-enforcing agencies, wine-making is regarded as an internal affair of the Hungarians. Other people "should not put their nose" into what is going on at home. Immigrants who are willing to adopt many other Canadian customs show a great reluctance to conform with the Canadian norms of drinking.

Birth Control

As an important characteristic in the life of the immigrants it should be mentioned that the small family prevailed in the sample group. Three out of every four families had only 1 to 3 children ever born, and only seven out of the ninety families had 5 or more. The average family in the sample was considerably smaller than the average Canadian family. According to the census of 1941, Canadian women ever married had on the average 3.3 children ever born. For the women in the sample group the rate was 2.5.[17] It is noteworthy that the difference between the two groups is smaller when children now living are considered: Canadian women having in 1941, 2.8, those in the sample group, 2.2.

The rather low birth rate in the sample cannot be regarded as representative for all Canadian Hungarians. There are many indications that Hungarian families in the Prairies, established by the old settlers, are larger than those of the sample. A similar decrease in the size of immigrant families other than Hungarian has been generally observed. The immigrants who came to America before 1910 had a high birth rate. After 1920, however, the birth rate of the foreign-born decreased. In 1940, in the United States, the birth rates of foreign-born women were almost exactly the same as those for native-born women. As the immigrants "have adopted American urban ways of living, their birth rates have dropped with astonishing rapidity."[18]

Small samples may yield misleading results concerning population movements. The interviews, however, gave sufficient evidence that

[17]Because of the remarriages of widowers, there were 93 mothers in the sample group. The three children born to these mothers out of their previous marriages were added to the number of children.

[18]Frank Lorimer and Frederick Osborn, *Dynamics of Population* (New York, 1934), p. 325; "Birth Rates among Foreign-Born No Longer above Average," *Statistical Bulletin*, Metropolitan Life Insurance Co., Nov. 1944.

birth control is generally practised in the group. Although no open questions were raised, casual remarks, made spontaneously by both men and women, gave relevant information on this point. Thus, one man speaking of his children said: "Then came [the youngest child] and we stopped." A woman puts the same idea as follows: "We have two children. Isn't that enough?" A third informant, speaking of a friend's family remarked: "The third child came accidentally." Undoubtedly, certain norms concerning the ideal size of the family were acknowledged by the immigrants, and husband and wife, with mutual consent, resorted to certain methods to restrict procreation.

Concerning the methods used, the practice of "free periods" in intercourse was well known by the European peasantry; among the immigrants it might be the old and most general means of restricting procreation. The members of the group are familiar with contraceptives, although they had been practically unknown by the rural proletariat in Hungary. Their use, however, is limited partly by moral considerations and partly by the difficulty of purchase. Immigrants in the Toronto area may easily obtain contraceptives through many outlets and particularly through special peddlers who sell them in factories and certain lunch bars. In a small town, however, a married immigrant uses contraceptives only when a friend purveys them from the city.

The main motive behind birth control is a socio-economic one. It was often said that the financial success of a family is preconditioned by birth control: "You can't make money enough for more children"; "In old times people had more children and less money." As another point of the same reasoning, it was generally understood that only by birth control can the children receive the necessary care and education. It was the opinion of the group that, because of birth control, their children are better cared for, better dressed, and better educated than those of certain other groups. As one woman put it: "Only the Jewish kids look better than ours." It would be hard to substantiate such a comparison, but it indicates that birth control became associated with national pride. It is not looked upon as a shame that should be hidden, but as proof of clever family policy—an attitude which characterized the rich peasantry in Hungary.

In twentieth-century Hungary, birth control figured as the foremost problem of public morality, a prominent issue in the press, in politics, and in literature. Birth control was practised by an increasing part of the population, but publicly condemned by state, church, and civic organizations. Its practice was particularly common in the middle class and in the rich peasantry. Birth control in the middle class is an international phenomenon. The situation in Hungary has not differed essentially from that in Germany or Sweden. The conditions prevailing among the rich peasantry were of local origin and influenced the behaviour of the immigrants.

In the agricultural system of Hungary, where all children shared the inheritance equally and where the large estate blocked the peasants' efforts to increase their farm holdings, the wealth of a rich peasant would have been dissipated at the first inheritance. To maintain wealth and status, a part of the peasantry, notably the Protestant ones, resorted to the one-child system. This type of birth control was observed as early as the 1880's,[19] and spread rapidly in the following decades. In the 1930's certain villages, with a long history of birth-control practice, were virtually dying out or were replenished by a poor Catholic population moving in from neighbouring localities.

The poor agrarian proletariat did not resort to contraceptive methods. Being not owners, but labourers, they had no financial considerations concerning heritage. On the contrary, they regarded children as a help, whose work or earnings would contribute to the precarious livelihood of the family. The typical Hungarian village was often described as one having few young people in the centre where the rich peasants lived, and many ragged, neglected, often hungry youngsters in the outskirts where the shacks of the have-nots were built.[20]

The immigrants of the sample group hailed from the large families of the poor class. They did not learn the practice of birth control from their parents, but adopted it in Canada, at about the same time as they became prosperous. In the decade 1920-9, 94 children were born in the families of the sample group; but the decade 1940-9 witnessed only 24 births, although the majority of the immigrants were of procreative age. Obviously, as the immigrants achieved financial success, they remembered the behaviour patterns of the rich peasantry in Hungary. The system of birth control had been known to them in the old country, but there it had not had any function for them. In the new country, with their fortune made, they adopted the practice in order to secure the prosperous status of the family. In other words, at the

---

[19]R. Temesváry, *Volksbräuche und Aberglaube in der Geburtshilfe in Ungarn* (Leipzig, 1900), quoted by William G. Sumner, *Folkways* (New York, 1907), § 323.

[20]Péter Elek *et al.*, *Elsülyedt falu a Dunántulon* (Budapest, 1936); János Hidvégi, *Hulló magyarság* (Budapest, 1938); Géza Kiss, *Ormányság* (Budapest, 1937); Béla Földes, "Influence de la situation matérielle et sociale sur les mariages, les naissances et les décès,"*Journal de la Société Hongroise de Statistique*, 1929.

time when the immigrant became successful in Canada, he adopted one important behaviour pattern from another Hungarian class.

Altogether, the mores of Hungarian immigrants are determined, in their essence, by old-country ideals, without any decisive Canadian influences. The immigrant is anxious not to collide with Canadian law and is proud of the good police record of his countrymen. Nevertheless, in the depth of his heart he does not approve of those facets of the Canadian normative code which differ from the corresponding Hungarian ones. He solves the conflict of two different value systems through small but workable compromises. His behaviour is regulated by three main principles: (1) It is not clever to break the law or oppose the mores of the new country. As the immigrants express it: "The police are always smarter than you." (2) That part of the Canadian normative code which coincides with the Hungarian one is approved. (3) In those cases where the Canadian and Hungarian norms collide, the immigrant approves the latter. His action, however, does not necessarily follow the Hungarian norms, but is determined by practical considerations. When the danger of repression is not imminent, he is prone to follow the Hungarian norms.

In his external form of life, the immigrant takes over the Canadian patterns, but his normative attitude strongly resists Canadian influences. The external form of life is tied up with success and material reward. Advertising, an ever present medium of communication, constantly educates and molds the immigrants' attitudes. It is the essence of competition that individuals must keep up, adapt themselves, and learn constantly under changing conditions. The normative system, on the other hand, is not directly linked to success or material reward. It is not influenced by agencies similar to advertising, and the ethnic churches and associations which could be factors in this field tend to perpetuate the old-country ideals.[21] Moreover, a normative attitude is a part of man's "character," formed in the years of youth and remaining stable and unaltered into old age. A man with "character" is not supposed to change his normative attitude with his residence. The adult immigrant brings along a finished character and a normative attitude formed in the old country. He is unwilling to change them and he experiences few promptings to do so. Normative values as they live within the Hungarian group reveal that part of the social heritage which has been least altered by Canadian influences.

[21]Y. J. Chyz and R. Lewis, "Agencies Organized by Nationality Groups in the United States," *Annals of the American Academy of Political and Social Science*, CCLXII (March 1949); V. J. Kaye, "Like Seeks Like," *Food for Thought*, Jan. 1953.

CHAPTER VII

CHALK ISLAND

THE PREVIOUS CHAPTERS have attempted to analyse the life of a Hungarian immigrant group in Canada. The analysis, however, covered only some of the group's activities; its presentation had to follow a certain logical sequence, thus dismembering the unity of real life and dissecting the procedure of personal adaptation. It is, therefore, necessary to reconstruct the process of adjustment in its real coherence.

The immigrant responds to the challenge of the land of choice with adjustment and assimilation. This response, however, is the outcome not of systematic planning, but of many trials and errors. Immigration and the establishment of a new existence in a strange country are momentous undertakings, necessarily tied up with many vicissitudes and hardships. It might be called fortunate that the immigrant, when making his great decision to leave his native country, is unaware of all the difficulties that lie ahead of him. He arrives in the new country with the belief that his life will be much the same as it was in the old country. He realizes only slowly, step by step, that the conditions in the land of choice are different. The discovery of differences between the old and new country creates, first of all, a certain bewilderment and timidity. As a second psychological reaction, an overcompensation may appear; the difficulties of the new life spur many immigrants to greater achievements. As one man put it: "I had to show that I am somebody too." The immigrant may or may not come to the conclusion that it is useful to adapt himself to the new conditions. But whether or not he approves it, the circumstances of the new country work on him from the moment of his arrival.

The changes that necessarily follow immigration interfere with all fields of life. They make up a coherent series in which every change is interrelated with other changes, and a single change often remains undistinguishable in practical life. For an average member of the sample group the process of change can be summed up as in Table VIII.

The entire process might be divided into two main parts. The first, what we call adjustment, witnesses all those changes that are neces-

TABLE VIII

SCHEME OF THE PROCESS OF ADJUSTMENT AND ASSIMILATION

SOCIAL HERITAGE			
	Psychological attitude	Success	Cultural field
ADJUSTMENT — Initiatory disorganization	Period of timidity and bewilderment General maladjustment: group disorganized, individual discontent	Ignorance of Canadian ways	
		Financial and occupational struggles	Visibly strange clothing, behaviour First orientations in Canada
		Collisions with law and other norms	
			Learning English and Canadian ways Fast adaptation to the external form of life
ADJUSTMENT — Transitory period	Achieving psychological security	Occupational adjustment Becomes competitor of full value	Slow changes in the family life
		Getting access to the "easy money" Period of saving	Discovery of the new country
ASSIMILATION — Mature immigrant group	Adjustment achieved: group socially stratified, individual finds his place in the status system of the group	Saturation point: the feeling of economic security	Canadian pretensions taken over Some conscious efforts to approach Canadian patterns
	Canada regarded as the second home Emotional attachment to Canadian details Feeling of equality	Partial competition with Canadians Respectable citizenry	English reading (newspapers) Some compromises in the normative values Canadian patriotism Partial identification with Canada Democratization
CANADIAN PATTERNS			

sary to make a living and to compete in the new society. During this time the immigrant comes into contact mainly with the external features of life in the new country, and the essence of these features often remains alien to him. His adjustment is prompted by circumstances, and he is pushed forward mainly by factors outside his will.

During the first years, the old- and new-country patterns clash, in the little world of the immigrant, rather dramatically. This is the background of that social disorganization which seems to be an unavoidable initiatory stage in the process of adjustment. When the immigrant acquires a certain orientation in the new country, he is able to integrate the clashing patterns; when he has successfully compromised the two patterns, the disorganization is ended. Of many compromises, those relating to economic activity are of paramount importance. The occupational adjustment makes him a competitor of full value and opens the way to the "easy money." After a period of successful saving he reaches a feeling of economic security. Now the conditions are favourable for him to take over Canadian pretensions which, again, push him further toward Canadian patterns.

The second main part in the series of changes, which follows that of adjustment in time, can be called assimilation. It is related to the non-material substratum of life. Adjustment leads the immigrant to successful competition; assimilation, to a more or less pronounced identification with the majority population. Assimilation, less conspicuous in its results than adjustment, manifests itself in the reading of English newspapers, in the acceptance of a certain form of Canadian patriotism, in a tendency toward respectable citizenry, and in a general democratization of the way of thinking.

In a mature immigrant group the members find their place in Canadian society, take over Canadian pretensions, feel an economic security, and make some conscious efforts to approach Canadian patterns. However, it is not a question of time alone to reach maturity. A great part of success depends on whether the changes in various fields occur at the right time, neither too early, nor too late. If the adaptation in clothing habits is too slow, the occupational adjustment and the financial success may be retarded. On the other hand, if Canadian pretensions are taken over too early, the saving plan of the family may suffer. For a successful adjustment, the changes must fit together like the gears of a complicated machine.

In the process of changes, the culture of the old country gradually disappears. A Hungarian priest in his sermon compared it to a chalk island which is constantly battered by the waves of the sea and diminishes bit by bit until it disappears from sight. The old-country patterns are washed away by the sea of Canadian experiences. As a matter of fact, the immigrant does not bring along a perfect copy of the old-country culture, but only some traits of it.[1] He can bring along only what he has. His social heritage is nothing but a random fragment of the local variation of the culture of his class, and it excludes many important aspects of the old-country culture. The Hungarian immigrant brought over what was the living culture of his home village and he had rather poor information about other parts of Hungarian culture.

For this reason, it is very unlikely that the social heritage of an immigrant group could be imposed upon the majority in the new country. There was a fear, expressed by Madison Grant and Lothrop Stoddard among others, that the cultural patterns of immigrants would finally corrupt the American culture. The heritage of the old country, however, is not vigorous enough to conquer new groups. It cannot maintain contact with the living culture of the old country; it lacks that social setting that could ensure its autonomous growth. The social heritage of immigrant groups becomes impoverished in the new country. As an example of this process, the language of the immigrants borrows many words and idioms from the English, but loses some parts of the mother tongue. The pidgin-Hungarian, as spoken by the members of the sample, is conspicuously poorer than the original language.[2]

The immigrant, actually, receives more in cultural patterns than he gives. He is invited to work, not to teach. American society has adopted only insignificant tidbits from the social heritage of immigrant groups; in most cases, culinary habits. Italians taught Americans to eat spaghetti; the Hungarians, goulash. Nor is the social heritage bequeathed to the children of the immigrants. Youths who grow up in America can adopt only that part of the old-country culture which is the living pattern in the parental home and which has survived the process of impoverishment. Second-generation people usually learn that pattern, but do not apply it in everyday life. Outside the parental home, they avail themselves of Canadian patterns and conform with the behaviour of their Canadian peer group. At the death of the parents, the practice of the old-country patterns is discontinued.

There cannot be much doubt that the disappearance of the social heritage was not always so rapid as it was observed to be in our

[1]Robert E. Park and Herbert Miller, *Old World Traits Transplanted* (New York, 1920).

[2]Joseph Remenyi, "Az amerikai magyar szellemi élet," and "A magyar nyelvü alkotó szellem lélektana Amerikában," *Magyar Szemle*, 1934 and 1937; John Kosa, "The Knowledge of English among Hungarian Immigrants," in I. Bernolak, A. R. Boyd, *et al.*, *Immigrants in Canada* (Montreal, 1955).

sample. The process of adjustment and assimilation shown by the sample seems to have taken place more rapidly than in those immigrant groups which were the subject of some earlier, authoritative studies.[3] There are, indeed, many indications that in our times the adjustment and assimilation of immigrants is more rapid and complete than it was some decades ago. Such a changed character of recent immigration can be explained by those changes which have occurred in both Hungarian and American society.

At the turn of the century, eastern and southern Europe, including Hungary, showed a conspicuous social and cultural lag when compared to western Europe and North America. In the following decades the cultural lag was, in many respects, narrowed down. The national societies of southeastern Europe, if not catching up, advanced rapidly. Education, urbanization, industrialization, and other important social changes affected all classes, including the poor ones.[4] A high percentage of those Hungarian immigrants who came at the turn of the century were illiterate, but after 1920 illiteracy was an exception.[5] The old immigrant at the turn of the century imagined his future as a wage earner in some industry involving hard manual work (mining, steel) and accepted the ups and downs of the labour market with natural resignation. The immigrant after 1920 brought with him an eager desire to participate in economic competition; he often went into some business of his own and showed a great mercantile spirit in buying and selling real estate. The modern immigrant appears to be more successful at adjustment and assimilation.[6]

At the same time momentous changes in American society transformed the milieu which received the immigrants. The immigrants arriving at the turn of the century had little chance of coming into contact with the native-born people. They huddled together in dense ethnic colonies. Immigrant and native-born lived far apart and any

[3]W. I. Thomas and Florian Znaniecki, *The Polish Peasant* (New York, 1927); Park and Miller, *Old World Traits Transplanted*; H. W. Zorbaugh, *The Gold Coast and the Slum* (Chicago, 1929); and, partly, W. Lloyd Warner and Leo Srole, *The Social Systems of American Ethnic Groups* (New Haven, 1945).

[4]Concerning the social changes in the peasantry see P. T. Bauer and John Kosa, *Az európai parasztság jövője* (Budapest, 1937); Péter Veres, *Az Alföld parasztsága* (Budapest, 1936); Ferenc Erdei, *Magyar falu* (Budapest, 1940), and *A. magyar paraszttársadalom* (Budapest, 1941); Julius Rezler, *A magyar nagyipari munkásság kialakulása* (Budapest, 1938); John Eppstein, ed., *Hungary* (Cambridge, 1945).

[5]Robert England, *The Central European Immigrant in Canada* (Toronto, 1929); W. Burton Hurd, "Racial Origins and Nativity of the Canadian People," *Seventh Census of Canada, 1931*, XIII, pp. 684–5.

[6]See Rudolf Heberle and Dudley S. Hall, *New Americans* (Baton Rouge, DP Commission, 1951); John C. Reed, "DP's Find Homes," *Social Order*, IV (Oct. 1954).

intercourse between them was restricted to the impersonal and superficial traffic of business. It was the era of laissez-faire policy when state and community interfered very little with the life of the individual. After 1920, however, the state, both in Canada and the United States, extended its activity to new areas touching upon the daily life of every citizen. Unemployment insurance in Canada, social security in the United States, and an elaborate taxation system had their effects even upon the immigrant. He became linked through important ties to the life of the national community. The rise of the labour movement was, from his point of view, even more momentous. Membership in a union tied the immigrant to a powerful organization in which he had rights and duties on an equal basis with the native-born. After 1930 it was impossible for the immigrant to live apart. He had to participate and interact in the national society.

As the laissez-faire policy was given up, American society definitely changed its attitude toward the immigrant. As professional social work was developed, special institutions were established to help him. Before 1930 he seldom encountered a helping agency, and if he did, it happened usually after he was deep in the troubles of social disorganization. Since the 1930's, social work and community organizations have systematically helped the immigrant in his adjustment, in personal or occupational difficulties, and in learning English.[7] Altogether it can be stated that attitudes in both Canada and the United States are now more favourable for the adjustment of immigrants than it was some decades ago.

The sample of our study, the members of which achieved success after many hardships, reflects the changed character of modern immigration. Both the unhappiness of the stranger and the chance of success await the arriving immigrant. With such an antithesis, his fate is a human one, the solution of which lies in his own hands. Those many immigrants who came from a country with strange customs and culture, who toiled, lived, raised children and met success not infrequently, are witnesses to the fact that the challenge of the land of choice can be solved in a human way. They established a new home and contributed their share to building both Canada and the United States. Their old-country culture disappeared as a chalk island in the sea. They themselves became Americanized, and in their families a new generation grew up which does not regard Canada any longer as a land of choice, but rather a native country—the natural home.

[7]Joseph Kage, "Immigration and Social Service," *Canadian Welfare*, March 1949; John P. Kidd, "Assimilation of New Canadians," address, July 2, 1952, Canadian Citizenship Council.

MEASURING ADJUSTMENT AND ASSIMILATION

THE ADJUSTMENT AND ASSIMILATION OF IMMIGRANTS represent a complex change in the general behaviour of individuals which manifests itself in the different fields of life. In the previous parts of the present study we tried to describe and interpret the changes in some selected fields. To complement the description, our research intended to measure those changes within the sample of 112 members, as well as some factors which may be instrumental in such a transition. For this quantitative analysis the following 13 measures were selected:

1. Financial success. The immigrants' success in financial fields (analysed in chapter III) was regarded as an indicator of his adjustment to the Canadian patterns of competition.

2. Marital success. As explained in chapter IV, the concept of marital happiness, elaborated and used in many sociological studies, is not directly connected with the special conditions created by immigration and adjustment. For our purpose, marital success was defined as the immigrant's ability to establish and maintain family life in Canada. Accordingly, the members of the sample were divided into two classes comprising 90 married men and 22 bachelors respectively.

3. Food preferences. As pointed out in chapter v, this was the only segment of the form of life that showed marked individual differences and could be used for measurement. The members were classified according to their predominant mode of cooking, and three food preferences (Canadian, Hungarian, and mixed) were established.

4. Knowledge of English. In the preliminary research we investigated how a group of Hungarian immigrants learned English.[1] The methods used there were applied to establish the knowledge of English acquired by the members of the sample.

5. Lack of feeling of discrimination. During the interviews 85 members of the group stated spontaneously that they experienced one or

[1]John Kosa, "The Knowledge of English among Hungarian Immigrants in Canada," in I. Bernolak, A. B. Boyd, et al., *Immigrants in Canada* (Montreal, 1955).

more instances of discrimination, while 27 members did not furnish voluntary complaints. On such a basis a threefold classification was made according to no complaint, one, and more than one case of voluntary complaints of discrimination.

6. Lack of group solidarity. This was measured by the immigrant's participation in formal ethnic organizations other than churches. The group was divided into three classes according to leadership, membership, and no membership in ethnic organizations.

7. Adjustment rating. A composite rating, based on the six previous measurements, was computed for each member. Point values from 0 to 5 were allotted for the achieved degree of adjustment in each field. Five points were given for the degree nearest to the Canadian patterns, 0 point for the degree nearest to the Hungarian patterns. By adding the points received on each measurement, the individual members could score an adjustment rating within the range from 0 to 30.

8. Satisfaction rating. For each group member two judges well acquainted with the member were selected from the ethnic group. They were asked whether the member was satisfied with his life in Canada. The answers were divided into three classes, and "undecided or conditional" was the classification for those cases where the judges disagreed or both gave conditional answers.

9. Liking for Canada. During the interviews the respondents made spontaneous statements commenting favourably or unfavourably on Canada. Such value judgments were distributed into three classes, "undecided" being used as the intermediate class.

10. Length of Canadian residence.

11. Urban residence.

12. Parental status. During the study many indications were found that children reared in Canada tend to act as mediators of the new-country culture. To test such a hypothesis, it was necessary to separate the families with children from the childless families and the bachelors.

13. Religious affiliation. An opinion (voiced by the general public rather than by sociologists) claims that similarity to the Anglo-Saxon cultural patterns in religious field promotes assimilation. Since the Hungarian is one of those peoples which are divided on the Catholic-Protestant line, the sample could be used to test such a hypothesis.

The first nine of the above mentioned measures indicate progress made in some field of life toward adjustment and assimilation; the last four measures refer to certain factors which might be hypothesized as promoting or retarding the process of adjustment. Out of the thirteen measures, however, only three (financial success, adjustment rating, length of Canadian residence) yield data which form continuous series.

For these three measures the Pearsonian coefficient was computed, and the results are summarized in Table IX. The data of the table show a significantly high correlation between financial success and adjustment rating, indicating that a financially successful person is

TABLE IX

r Values for Three Variables

	(1)	(7)	(10)
(1) Financial success			
(7) Adjustment rating	.71		
(10) Length of Canadian residence	.19	.14	

likely to make adjustment in some other fields of life too. On the other hand, the length of Canadian residence does not show any significant correlation with financial success and adjustment rating. It should be remembered, however, that the sample was made up of immigrants who had been in Canada for more than fifteen years. It is very likely that in a mature immigrant group, such as in the sample, the individual variations are more important than those which can be attributed to the varying length of Canadian residence.

Most measures enumerated above could not be conceived as "variables" which give continuous series, but as "categories" which yield discrete data and cannot be used for computing the Pearsonian coefficient. In order to obtain data from these measures (data which are comparable within certain limits) it was necessary to resort to a method less reliable than the product-moment coefficient. For such a purpose the contingency (square means) coefficient was used. Accordingly, all the thirteen measures were divided into appropriate classes, and the class distribution was used for computing the C values through an application of Yates's correction for continuity as well as the correction recommended by Yule and Kendall for comparability.[2] Table X shows the corrected contingency correlations (C_{cor}) for the thirteen measures. Although the results are presented in matrix form, they are not product-moment correlations and cannot be used for further operations such as factor analysis.

Table X gives some useful information. It shows, for example, that Catholic religious affiliation is significantly correlated with only one other measure, the lack of group solidarity. Thus, it might be assumed

[2] F. Yates, "Contingency Tables Involving Small Numbers," *Supplement to Journal of the Royal Statistical Society*, I (1934); G. Udny Yule and M. G. Kendall, *An Introduction to the Theory of Statistics* (14th ed., London, 1950), chap. III.

TABLE X

CONTINGENCY CORRELATIONS OF 13 MEASURES

	1.	2.	3.	4.	5.	6.	7.	8.	9.	10.	11.	12.	13.
1. Financial success													
2. Marital success	.75**												
3. Food preference	.17	.30											
4. Knowledge of English	.30	.16	.21										
5. No feeling of discrimination	.34*	.38*	.15	.40									
6. Lack of group solidarity	.42	.36	.26	.22	.13								
7. Adjustment rating	.45**	.78**	.47*	.36	.41*	.31							
8. Satisfaction rating	.72**	.58**	.38	.32	.43*	.36	.69**						
9. Liking for Canada	.53**	.31	.41*	.26	.29	.25	.46*	.53**					
10. Length of Canadian residence	.42	.20	.38	.30	.16	.43	.26	.31	.37				
11. Urban residence	.22	.28	.52**	.23	.20	.16	.35	.17	.20	.32			
12. Parental status	.64**	.92**	.42*	.37	.37*	.42	.55**	.68**	.56**	.22	.19		
13. Religious affiliation	.10	.16	.22	.19	.27	.45*	.21	.39	.25	.30	.41	.38	

*p > .01
**p > .001

that religious affiliation in itself is not a decisive factor in the assimilation of Hungarian immigrants.

In order to interpret the correlations of the measures, a profile analysis was prepared, and the probability of the correlations examined. Regarding those correlations that have a probability of .01 or better as significant, the profile analysis permitted the following interpretation:

Six measures (financial and marital success, adjustment and satisfaction rating, liking for Canada, and parental status) show a similar behaviour on the correlation profile and seem to point to a common basis. Generally speaking it might be stated that those immigrants who achieve financial and marital success show a good adjustment rating indicating that they are approaching the Canadian patterns in some other aspects of behaviour as well, seem to be satisfied in their new country, like Canada, and enjoy a parental status. In other words, success is likely to go along with adjustment in some other fields too.

Two other measures (food preferences, lack of feeling of discrimination) differ in their correlation profile and do not seem to be closely connected with the common basis of the previous six measurements. Nevertheless, they show certain correlations with some of the above mentioned six measures. The independent behaviour of food preferences and feeling of discrimination might be attributed to various factors which are not measured in the present study and which are not necessarily connected with other fields of adjustment. The food preferences of a family, for example, may be determined by the mother's employment outside the household.

Finally, five measures (knowledge of English, lack of group solidarity, length of Canadian residence, urban residence,[3] and religion) are not correlated with the other eight measures and seem to be affected by circumstances other than those which affect financial and marital success. In other words, success in life does not necessarily go along with good English, with a specific attitude toward the ethnic group, with a certain religious affiliation, or with a long residence in Canada.[4]

[3]Urban residence shows one significant correlation, with food preferences, which might be explained by the fact that farmers and other rural people tend to retain the Hungarian food patterns.

[4]In another study, based on the Canadian census, the author made an attempt to determine some factors in the assimilation of immigrants of various ethnic origins ("Factors in the Assimilation of Ethnic Groups in Canada," in manuscript). The measures used in the two studies are not entirely comparable, but within a limited range the two findings seem to be corroborative.

The complex changes represented by adjustment and assimilation cannot be explained by one factor or circumstance, but are very likely affected by all those factors or circumstances which touch upon the life of the immigrant. Complex as such a social field might be, it nevertheless shows certain regularities. One of them is the relative importance of success in the immigrant's life, and the other is the relative unimportance of such circumstances as the length of Canadian residence, urban or rural residence, and religious affiliation.

Index

Lightning Source UK Ltd.
Milton Keynes UK
UKHW012359200722
406167UK00001B/296